Karen Drake's

Book of Hope

A Theopathic Guide

To Health and Healing

By

Karen E. Drake, TMD., D.MIN.

Karen Drake's Book of Hope
Copyright © 2011, 2020 by Karen E. Drake
ALL RIGHTS RESERVED

Except as permitted under the US copyright act of 1976, no part of this publication may be reproduced, distributed, or transmitted in any form or by any means, or stored in a database retrieval system without the prior written permission of the publisher.

Unless otherwise indicated, all Scripture quotations are taken from the *Holy Bible, King James Version*, public domain. References marked NKJV are from The Holy Bible, New King James Version, copyright © 1979, 1980, 1982, Thomas Nelson, Inc., Nashville, Tennessee. References marked AMPC are from *The Amplified Bible, Classic Edition*, copyright © 1954, 1958, 1962, 1964, 1965, 1987 by The Lockman Foundation, La Habra, California. References marked NIV are from the *Holy Bible, New International Version*, copyright © 1973, 1978, 1984 by International Bible Society, Colorado Springs, Colorado. References marked "NLT" are from *The Holy Bible, New Living Translation*, copyright © 1996, 2004, 2007 by Tyndale House Foundation. Used by permission of Tyndale House Publishers, Inc., Carol Stream, Illinois. References marked "CEB" are from *The Common English Bible*, copyright © 2011 by Common English Bible, Nashville, Tennessee. References marked MSG are from *THE MESSAGE*, copyright © 1993, 1994, 1995, 1996, 2000, 2002 by NavPress Publishing Group, Colorado Springs, Colorado.

The entire contents of this book are based upon research conducted by the author, unless otherwise noted. The publisher, author, distributors and bookstores present this information for educational purposes only. This information is not intended to diagnose or prescribe for medical or psychological conditions, nor does it claim to prevent, treat, mitigate or cure such conditions nor to recommend specific information, products or services as treatments of disease nor to provide diagnosis, care, treatment or rehabilitation of individuals, or applied medical, mental health or human development principles, to provide diagnosing, treating, operating or prescribing for any human disease, pain, injury, deformity or physical condition. The information contained herein is not intended to replace a one-on-one relationship with your doctor or qualified healthcare professional. Therefore, the reader should be made aware that this information is not intended as medical advice, but rather a sharing of knowledge and information from the research and experience of the author. Testimonials represent a cross section or range of results that appear to be typical with the information, products or services. Results may vary depending upon use and commitment. This information is intended solely for expressive association purposes. The publisher and author encourage you to make your own healthcare decisions based upon your research and in partnership with a qualified healthcare professional. You and you alone are responsible if you choose to do anything based upon what you read here.

Published by

Primus Press and Publications
Box 86054
Phoenix, AZ 85080
www.PrimusUniversityofTheology.com
email: Info@PrimusUniversityofTheology.com

Cover design by Carrie and Win Wachsmann

ISBN 978-0-9834463-1-6

Printed on demand
For Worldwide Distribution

Dedication

First and foremost, I dedicate this book to my heavenly Father, without whom I could not have survived my battle with breast cancer. He gave me the willpower and perseverance to continue searching for a natural approach to beat cancer and restore my body to health. His Word assured me that He would give me wisdom in my search.

If any of you lack wisdom, let him ask of God, who giveth to all men liberally and upbraideth not, and it shall be given him. James 1:5

Ezekiel spoke of God's intention for the trees and plants He created:

The fruit thereof shall be for food and the leaf thereof for medicine. Ezekiel 4:7

My experience taught me what the apostle Paul meant in his letter to the Philippians:

I can do all things through Christ which strengtheneth me. Philippians 4:13

Without the strength I received through my faith in Christ I fear I would have been overwhelmed by the magnitude of doubt and skepticism constantly challenging me to take the contemporary medical approach rather than to seek the natural way to health. By His grace and mercy, I was healed.

Second, to the memory of my precious late husband, Richard, who respected and defended my decision to treat cancer with a holistic approach. He encouraged me to stand on what I believed and prayerfully stood with me day after day throughout those long and frustrating two years, as we battle, not only the cancer, but also those who thought I was insane to disobey the medical doctors. It was through his insistence that I journaled my experiences and the miraculous ways in which God moved to restore my health, and this led to the book being written.

Finally, my deepest gratitude to all those who prayed for me to recover. It was their faith and encouragement that gave me hope. As the Bible instructs:

James 5:14
> *Is any sick among you? let him call for the elders of the church; and let them pray over him, anointing him with oil in the name of the Lord.*

I never would have known how many friends I had and how deeply their love went if I had not been challenged with cancer. They offered not only physical strength, but also financial support when necessary. If I hadn't put my life and recovery in God's hands, I would have missed out on all of those miracles.

God laid it on the hearts of dear friends, John and Sharon, Jim and Nellie and Bobby and Virginia Parker to help financially when I had no other means. God miraculously made me aware of Sanoviv, a medical facility in Mexico, where I received treatment, and laid it upon the heart of our friends, John and Sharon, to fund my treatment there.

God put the right people into my life just when I needed them: Joyce Rathburn at Sanoviv, who encouraged me to read Psalms 27, which assured me that even if everyone else would forsake me, then the Lord would take care of me:

Psalm 27:14, NKJV
Wait on the Lord;
be of good courage,
And He shall strengthen your heart;
wait, I say, on the Lord!

Last, but certainly not least, God arranged for me to receive treatment at Sanoviv when Jon and Esther were there. He also laid it on their hearts to volunteer to pay for my surgery and the additional expenses of the vitamins and supplements that I would need during my recovery. I will never forget the humbling feeling of having so many care so deeply for me. Such love I could never have imagined. Thank you all!

Accolades

Deepest gratitude to my loving family:

My parents, Robert and Eileen Cook, raised me in a Christian home and saw to it that I was educated at St. John's Lutheran School in Arnold, Missouri. There, I learned to trust in God—Father, Son, and Holy Spirit—Who became my constant Companion and best Friend. My faith in God and appreciation for His blessings instilled in me as a child sustained me through this life-threatening illness.

My father loves the outdoors. He taught me to fish from the creek bank, hunt the woods for wild mushrooms and the pastures for blackberries. He taught me to appreciate being alone in the silent beauty of nature and respect all that God provided for our nourishment and enjoyment.

My mother always tried a natural approach before racing off to a physician for every little ailment. She used a hot rag for an earache and ice for a burn, teaching me the simple truth that natural cures can be administered safely and effectively at home.

My paternal grandparents, Walter Emory and Nora Cook, depended on the bounty of the land to sustain them. I will always remember the trips to the meadow where Grandma selected wild plants for our dinner and the hours she spent picking out wild hickory nuts for her wonderful baked goods. Also, the time spent with Grandpa, fishing from the creek bank, tending to his animals, and listening to his stories of times past, while he barbecued over an open fire. These experiences left an indelible impression on me, imparting an appreciation for God's natural provision.

There were also my maternal grandparents, Theodore and Ruth Noll, on whose farm I had the good fortune of being raised. Their long days spent working in the fields, raising crops for a living, taught me the value of hard work and the importance of family and enveloped me with an unalterable sense of security. I will never forget the fragrance of the freshly-tilled earth, the delight in eating vegetables right in the field where they had grown, or the smells of the harvest. Never was a meal eaten without thanking God for His bounty and provision. Nor would a day go by without experiencing the beauty of God's creation. These are treasures that sustain me.

Acknowledgments

There were many people who encouraged the writing of this book, but there are several to whom I must give special recognition and thanks.

First, my late husband, Richard, who, more than anyone else, saw the vision of "hope" my experience could offer others afflicted with a life-threatening illness. He, therefore, diligently encouraged me to record what I had learned during this experience and instructed me in the wisdom, strength and comfort offered throughout the Word of God.

Second, Barbara Watts, of Quick Study, Good Friends, Inc., has indeed been a gift from God. She offered to edit this work and committed countless hours of her precious time critiquing it. It is through her devotion and creative genius that my experience has been transformed into a publishable work.

Finally, my beloved friends and neighbors—Mrs. Ethel Meals, Demetra Foster, Maurice Craig and Jeanne Muriah—for their time devoted to proofreading and the priceless hours spent encouraging me throughout the entire process.

Disclaimer

Any references to Phoenix University School of Theology (PHXUT) in this book refer to the name of the university and vision for the university given by God to Dr. Richard Drake, Founder. This should not be confused with the University of Phoenix. The university Richard founded has since changed its name to Primus University of Theology International in order to prevent any further confusion.

FOR YE ARE ALL THE CHILDREN OF GOD BY FAITH IN CHRIST JESUS.

Galatians 3:26

Contents

Introduction 15

1. Miracles at Sanoviv 21
2. A Day I Will Never Forget 42
3. The Role of Healing Prayers 57
4. Treatment Decisions 61
5. Overcoming the Skepticism of Many 70
6. What I Did and Why I Did It 74
   - My Daily Regimen 75
   - Homeopathic Remedies 80
   - Botanical Herbs 80
   - Drainage 81
   - Foods and Their Health Benefits 83
7. Understanding Your Body 89
8. The Role of Our Mental Attitude in Healing 99
9. The Role of Diet in Healing 107
10. The Role of Abstinence in Healing 114
11. The Role of Wine and Spirits in Healing ... 120
12. The Dangers Posed by Food Additives 124
13. The Role of Water in Healing 131
14. The Role of Exercise in Healing 139
15. The Role of Sunlight in Healing 144

16. The Role of Rest in Healing 150
17. The Role of Meditation in Healing 155
18. Understanding Our Body's pH Level 159
19. The Necessary Dental Focus......................166
20. The Benefits of a Coffee Enema Cleanse..171
21. In Closing 175

    Resources..176
    Author Contact Page....................................179

Introduction

Even as a child, I always wanted to help others. I felt compelled to make everyone I encountered smile, to bring some joy or gladness to their day. For a long time I actually believed my mother and father named me Karen because I was to be a caring (Kar'en) person.

I dreamed of becoming a missionary, then thought of being a teacher. Circumstances, however, prevented my educational dreams from materializing ... until my life's experiences, both the highs and the lows, prepared me to follow my dreams.

For many years, I satisfied my desire to help others and make a difference in the world by working in the medical field while tithing my income to help those less fortunate. God's Word is very specific about tithing.

Deuteronomy 12:16, AMPC
> *You shall bring your...tithes and the offering of your hands, and your vows and your freewill offerings, and the firstlings of your herd and of your flock.*

Malachi also warned us what to expect if we do not tithe:

Malachi 3:7-9, AMPC
Return to me, and I will return to you, says the L*ord* *of hosts. But you say, How shall we return? Will a man rob or defraud God? ... But you say, In what way do we rob or defraud You? [You have withheld your] tithes and offerings. You are cursed with the curse, for you are robbing Me, even this whole nation.*

I was convinced that we were to use our lives and our income for more than our own existence and pleasure. Colossians 3:12-17 describes how we ought to live our lives:

Colossians 3:12-17, NKJV
Therefore, as the elect of God, holy and beloved, put on tender mercies, kindness, humility, meekness, longsuffering; bearing with one another, and forgiving one another, if anyone has a complaint against another; even as Christ forgave you, so you also must do. But above all these things put on love [charity], which is the bond of perfection. And let the peace of God rule in your hearts, to which also you were called in one body; and be thankful. Let the word of Christ dwell in you richly in all wisdom, teaching and admonishing one another in psalms and hymns

Introduction

and spiritual songs, singing with grace in your hearts to the Lord. And whatever you do in word or deed, do all in the name of the Lord Jesus, giving thanks to God the Father through Him.

When I was working as a medical assistant, there was always a gnawing in my spirit that I was just not doing enough. I tried to encourage others and share the Word of God, praying with patients and putting inspirational scriptures on every patient's receipts each day. Then, one day, I came across a message in my daily inspirational calendar that touched my spirit. I began to pray it every day: "LORD, HELP ME TO FULFILL MY POTENTIAL." Jesus said:

Matthew 7:7
Ask and it shall be given you; seek, and ye shall find; knock and it shall be opened unto you.

I believed God would direct my path for His Word promised that He would.

One Monday morning in late August of 1998, I was awakened hearing a voice saying, "Be a doctor." I felt that God was answering my prayer by directing my path. I had never been to college or taken the college entrance examination. Now, in middle-age, it seemed an unlikely possibility. However, I felt so strongly about what I had just heard that I went that very morning and signed up for classes at a nearby college—Union University in Jackson, Tennessee.

God is great! Not only was I accepted into the pre-med program, but the classes actually started that very night! My counselor scheduled my college placement tests for the following Saturday. Amazingly, after being away from school for so many years, I passed the tests! It was awesome how God opened the doors and helped me step through them when I followed His instructions.

In order to complete my bachelor's program as quickly as possible, I moved to St. Louis, Missouri, and stayed with my Aunt Alice, taking accelerated courses at Logan Chiropractic College. I had heard of a new program being offered in Phoenix, Arizona, at the College of Integrative Medicine. This program offered combined courses in medical and naturopathic studies, and I wanted to be one of the first to enroll. I was on a mission and had no time to waste!

After the first semester at the College of Integrative Medicine, I realized that my desire (and, I believe, my calling) was to focus more on health and healing through natural means than on the standard medical and pharmacological approach. Because of that, I transferred to Southwest Naturopathic College in Tempe, Arizona, to continue my studies.

While attending school in Arizona, I married an amazing man. He was a minister, teacher and

Introduction

theologian. I had never met anyone quite like Richard Drake! He was awesome! His unwavering faith in God and total commitment to serving the Lord, coupled with his deep understanding of the Word of God and compassion for his fellowman, inspired me so much that I actually prayed to be like him.

My marriage caused me to reevaluate my educational goals. Once again, I changed my focus, this time to Theology, majoring in the healing principals directed by the Scriptures. Paul admonished his spiritual son Timothy:

2 Timothy 2:15
Study to shew thyself approved unto God, a workman that needeth not to be ashamed, rightly dividing the word of truth.

Now I knew that I was on the right track and on the way to fulfilling my potential!

In 2003, I received my Master's Degree in Ministry from Phoenix Theological Seminary (now Primus), then went on to attain my Doctorate in Theopathic Health and Healing in 2008, again from Phoenix University of Theology (now Primus).

This unique course of study teaches Christian, spiritual, biblical and natural perspectives on health and healing. The focus is on the natural healing process: walking in God's healing power, embracing a life of divine health, and having a greater impact and influence on one's own path to health and healing God's Way. It worked for me when I was diagnosed with cancer.

Karen Drake
Phoenix, Arizona

CHAPTER 1

Miracles at Sanoviv

During most of 2006, my battle with breast cancer consisted of natural approaches to treatment in the belief that my body was designed by God to heal itself if given the proper nutrition, diet, and exercise, along with the proper mental attitude. The Word of God tells us to pray and have faith in the healing grace of our Lord and Savior Jesus Christ, because it is through His grace (not our works), that we are saved. As Paul wrote to the Ephesians and to Timothy:

Ephesians 2:8
For by grace are ye saved through faith; and that not of yourselves: it is the gift of God,

2 Timothy 1:9
Who hath saved us, and called us with an holy calling, not according to our works, but according to

his own purpose and grace, which was given us in Christ Jesus before the world began ... .

I had discovered the lump in January and began doing everything I could afford to restore my body to health. By November, however, the tumor was still detectable.

Richard and I were out of money, unable to continue purchasing the expensive vitamins and supplements that had been so much a part of my treatment. We decided, even though our resources were limited, that I should take one final trip to Melbourne, Florida, to see Dr. Jonathan Clark and get a reading on how the cancer was responding.

The report was encouraging! My body was obviously reacting favorably to everything I was doing. The tumor had shrunk from the size of my thumb to the size of the tip of my little finger! But, it was still there, and there was no more money to purchase products to fight it.

I had confessed my healing; now I had to believe (even though things looked a little bleak at the moment) that my recovery was completely in God's hands. The writer to the Hebrews declared:

Hebrews 13:5
... Be content with such things as ye have: for he hath said, I will never leave thee, nor forsake thee.

It wasn't until all our financial resources were exhausted that I stopped trying to find the cure and put my total faith in God. There is no doubt that everything I did was beneficial to my recovery, but in the end, it was all God! It was time that I trusted totally in Him and not my research or financial resources.

I prayerfully spent every available moment in Florida walking on the warm sandy beaches, soaking up the balmy sun's rays, and enjoying the wonderful ocean breeze for the last time. I knew this was the final stage of treatment as I had known it. Richard was back in Tennessee praying for God's guidance, while I was in Florida praying the same, both of us assured that God would show us the way. Jesus assured us:

Matthew 18:19
Again I say unto you, That if two of you shall agree on earth as touching any thing that they shall ask, it shall be done for them of my Father which is in heaven.

What an awesome God we serve! By the time I returned home, our prayers had been answered. While I was in Florida, John, a close friend, had called and told Richard the incredible story of a man and his wife he had encountered by chance on three different occasions while lecturing in Ohio. He said that after the third encounter he had come to feel that God was trying to show him something, and he thought of me.

The woman in question had terminal cancer and had been put on morphine and sent home to die. Unwilling to accept this death sentence, her husband had equipped a private plane and flown her to a hospital in Mexico where, he had learned, they were using alternative treatments for cancer patients and claiming remarkable results. The result, for this couple, was that the wife went home from that treatment after only two weeks free of cancer! John was asking if Richard would like to have the couple's phone number so that we could talk to them directly.

Just as John was giving Richard the phone number, he saw the couple approaching him in the hotel and offered the phone to them so that they could speak directly with Richard. Their story was very encouraging ... except for one thing: the treatment in Mexico was expensive, and we were out of money.

After arriving home in Dallas, John shared his story with his lovely wife, Sharon, and they felt led to help us financially. John informed Richard that they were sending a check to cover the trip and two weeks of treatment.

The promise of God in Luke 6:38 is: *"I shall cause men to give into your bosom."* Sure enough, God had made a way when there seemed to be no way, just as the song says:

Miracles at Sanoviv

God Will Make A Way[1]

God will make a way,
Where there seems to be no way.
He works in ways we cannot see.
He will make a way for me.
He will be my guide,
Hold me closely to His side.
With love and strength for each new day.
He will make a way. He will make a way.

By a roadway in the wilderness, He'll lead me.
And rivers in the desert will I see.
Heaven and earth will fade,
But His Word will still remain.
He will do something new today.

Proverbs declares:

Proverbs 3:6

In all thy ways acknowledge him, and he shall direct thy paths.

God put this couple with their amazing testimony into John's life at just the right moment. Then He laid it on John's heart to pay the thousand-dollar-a-day treatment for me. It is magnificent how God so profoundly answered our prayers, in His own timing and in His own unique way.

1. Lyrics and Music by Don Moen © Capitol Christian Music Group

I knew in my heart and soul that this was going to be the treatment that cured me. So, I thanked God with every ounce of my strength and told everyone I met about His answer to our prayers. I was on Cloud Nine, confident that this was all God-ordained. As Chronicles instructs us:

1 Chronicles 16:8
Give thanks unto the Lord, call upon his name, make known his deeds among the people.

Several days before I was to leave for Mexico, I had a dream about being at the hospital, but it seemed more like a dingy, barren fortress—all enclosed and frightening. Apparently, I was a bit more apprehensive about the trip than I had realized, for my mind to have conjured up such a thought. I was inspired by remembering the scripture from Joshua:

Joshua 1:7-9
… Be thou strong and very courageous, … that thou mayest prosper withersoever thou goest. This book … thou shalt meditate therein day and night, that thou mayest observe to do according to all that is written therein: for then thou shalt make thy way prosperous, and then thou shalt have good success. Have not I commanded thee? Be strong and of a good courage; be not afraid, neither be thou dismayed: for the Lord thy God is with thee whithersoever thou goest.

The very next night I had another dream. Again, I was at the hospital. This time, it was like a beautiful mansion—pristine and bright. I was in front of a marvelous estate, saying farewell to an elegant lady, and it appeared that we had been close friends. As we hugged goodbye, she said that she wanted to adopt me, but I would need to change my name to Rosemary Rothschild. I remember waking up at that moment and saying out loud, "Rosemary Rothschild," and feeling empowered by such an elegant name.

The Bible tells us that God speaks to us in dreams and visions. He assures us He is our God, and everything is His:

Psalm 50:7-15
> *Hear, O my people, and I will speak; ... I am God, even thy God ... For every beast of the forest is mine, and the cattle upon a thousand hills. ... for the world is mine, and the fullness thereof ... call upon me in the day of trouble: I will deliver thee, and thou shalt glorify me.*

What peace to know that God, our heavenly Father, has limitless resources, and, therefore, we, as His heirs, have the same.

Romans 8:15, NLT

> ... *You have not received a spirit that makes you fearful slaves. Instead, you received God's Spirit when he adopted you as his own children. Now we call him, Abba, Father.*

Isaiah declared that we will receive a new name:

Isaiah 62:2

> *And thou shalt be called by a new name, which the mouth of the LORD shall name.*

Galatians speaks directly about our inheritance:

Galatians 4:4-7

> *... God sent forth his Son ... to redeem them that were under the law, that we might receive the adoption of sons. And because ye are sons, God hath sent forth the Spirit of his Son into your hearts, crying, Abba, Father. Wherefore thou art no more a servant, but a son; and if a son, then an heir of God through Christ.*

As children of God, we need not worry; we need only believe as Jesus said:

Mark 9:23

> *Jesus said unto him, If thou canst believe, all things are possible to him that believeth.*

Miracles at Sanoviv

Our friend John was financing the hospital expenses, and God continued to provide for the rest of our needs by encouraging others to give of their resources. We have the promise of Jesus:

Luke 6:38
> *Give, and it shall be given unto you; good measure, pressed down, and shaken together, and running over, shall men give into your bosom. For with the same measure that ye mete withal it shall be measured to you again.*

The airfare for the trip to Mexico was made possible by my parents with a $1,500 Christmas gift, and our church took up a collection of $1,400, which supplied all the rest of what was needed to get to the hospital. I believed that whatever happened on this trip was the will of God, and He was ordering the circumstances. Jesus's teachings in Matthew 6 tell us to take life one day at a time and leave the cares of the world to God:

Matthew 6:25-34
> *Therefore I say unto you, Take no thought for your life, what ye shall eat, or what ye shall drink; nor yet for your body, what ye shall put on. Is not the life more than meat, and the body than raiment? Behold the fowls of the air: for they sow not, neither do they reap, nor gather into barns; yet your heavenly Father feedeth them. Are ye not much better than they?*

Which of you by taking thought can add one cubit unto his stature?
And why take ye thought for raiment? Consider the lilies of the field, how they grow; they toil not, neither do they spin: and yet I say unto you, That even Solomon in all his glory was not arrayed like one of these. Wherefore, if God so clothe the grass of the field, which today is, and tomorrow is cast into the oven, shall he not much more clothe you, O ye of little faith?
Therefore take no thought, saying, What shall we eat? or, What shall we drink? or, Wherewithal shall we be clothed? For your heavenly Father knoweth that ye have need of all these things. But seek ye first the kingdom of God, and his righteousness; and all these things shall be added unto you. Take therefore no thought for the morrow: for the morrow shall take thought for the things of itself. Sufficient unto the day is the evil thereof.

My flight landed in San Diego, California, on Tuesday, January 23, 2007—just two days short of a year from the day I had first found the lump in my breast. I had come a long way since my oncologist, in essence, had pronounced my six-month death sentence. From San Diego, the Sanoviv shuttle drove me the thirty-mile trip to Santa Rosa, just south of Tijuana.

The travel was made much easier by the fact that the hospital had instructed me to bring nothing with me, no extra clothes, no shoes, no cosmetics and no toiletries. They would provide everything, just as Jesus said: *"Take no thought for your life, what ye shall eat, or what ye shall drink; nor yet for your body, what ye shall put on."* I was living out His words.

Since I had not done a great deal of traveling outside of the United States, the trip through Customs and into Mexico was a bit intimidating. People were not very friendly, and since I don't speak Spanish, I felt vulnerable. I survived.

As we pulled into the garrison-looking, walled hospital and stopped at the huge iron gates and waited for the guard to allow us access, I had a flashback to my first dream and imagined the prison-type environment that might be awaiting me inside those walls. But, praise the Lord, the second dream was more accurate!

As the shuttle passed through the gates, which quickly closed behind us, I observed a beautiful stucco facility with more windows than walls, and it was all encompassed in an elegant garden setting, complete with waterfalls, stone walkways, statuary and magnificent flowers and greenery. I had heard about extravagant, luxury hospitals where the rich and famous went for rest and healing. Well, this was one of those places!

The main building had originally been Levi Strauss' sprawling marble mansion, situated on the rocky cliffs overlooking the Pacific. It had been transformed into a luxury hospital but had kept its sense of affluence and attention to detail.

The initial tour and registration process was thorough but lacking any real sense of warmth. Everyone seemed very professional and all-business. Since I had been raised in a large and affectionate family and now lived in a small town in Tennessee (where I knew all my neighbors), this place seemed rather cold. I felt like I needed a hug.

After registration, I was shown to my suite. It was gorgeous ... well, at least the view was gorgeous. The balcony overlooked the Pacific, and the splendidly landscaped pool and spa areas were just below my window. I loved it! The bedroom drawers were filled with everything I was to wear, and the bathroom was fully stocked with all the necessary toiletries. I understood the concept that in this controlled environment everyone wore the same thing, to avoid any sensitivity or reaction to fabrics, detergents or perfumes. But, somehow, it seemed a little bit like a Twilight Zone movie, with everyone dressed identically.

I changed into tan cotton sweats and therapeutic sandals and went to the main floor to start my treatments. There was a pleasant waiting area in the main lobby where everyone congregated as they waited to be escorted by the physicians and therapists to whatever treatment they would be receiving that day. They didn't let us wait long, so there wasn't much time to get to know other patients.

My first day was fairly awkward. It actually took about twenty-four hours before I understood the routine and learned where everything was located. I decided to make it my personal quest to prevent anyone else from having such an uncomfortable first day, so I greeted every new patient and familiarized them with the things that had baffled me initially. It wasn't that difficult to meet everyone, since I have never met a stranger, and the hospital only accommodated forty patients at any one time.

That Wednesday evening, permission had been given for the patients to hold a prayer meeting in the library. The result was that the atmosphere throughout the entire hospital changed. Everyone was excited about getting together. It was as if God had planned for these particular Christians to be together at the hospital at the same time, praising and worshiping Him, lending strength and encouragement to each other.

Jon and Esther began the meeting with a scripture reading and prayer. Then we all sang hymns and prayed for one another. Everyone told their particular story, and we all became instant family.

Jesus said:

Matthew 12:50
For whosoever shall do the will of my Father which is in heaven, the same is my brother, and sister, and mother.

From that point on, even the physicians and therapists prayed and discussed scripture during our treatments.

The hospital was great. Every patient had a schedule for their daily activities, and the appointments flowed like a finely-tuned machine. There was little, if any, waiting time.

Each day began at six a.m. with a warm cup of lemon water and cayenne pepper. Half an hour later, we took four ounces of wheat grass. Then we were off to exercise class and meditation before breakfast, which consisted of oats, nuts and fruit.

The morning hours were spent with testing and lab work, and then came lunch. Afternoons were spent in therapy, some of it more enjoyable than others—like massage, facials, manicures, saunas and pool time.

Dinner was served promptly at six. The meals were all served buffet-style, with all the salad, sprouts, and seeds one could possibly eat and, of course, handsful of vitamins.

Evenings were reserved for lectures and instructional classes. Finally, there was one more therapy session, and then we were off to bed by 10:15.

Over the course of several days, I had extensive diagnostic testing, lab work, X-rays and more therapies than I could count. On Friday, the test results were in, and the physicians were ready with their medical evaluations. I expected them to tell me that the diet, supplements and treatment they were providing would cure the cancer. I was disheartened when they recommended surgical removal of the cancerous tumor. I knew that God had arranged the circumstances that had gotten me to Sanoviv, and I believed He would continue to provide whatever was necessary for my healing.

I told the physician my story of how a friend sponsored my treatment and that I had no money for surgery. He explained why the tumor needed to be removed, told me the exact cost of the surgery ($13,950), and said he would continue with the treatment schedule as originally outlined and pray for the best.

That evening I called Richard and told him of the physicians' recommendation for surgery. My husband was awesome; his faith never wavered. He assured me that he was confident that God would make a way if surgery was indeed what I needed. Together we prayed for God's will to be done and that He would strengthen my faith.

We recalled the words of Hebrews:

Hebrews 11:1 and 6
Now faith is the substance of things hoped for, the evidence of things not seen.
But without faith it is impossible to please him: for he that cometh to God must believe that he is, and that he is a rewarder of them that diligently seek him.

After speaking with Richard, I also called my parents to let them know how the treatment was going and to tell them that the physician recommended surgery at a cost of $13,950. They were skeptical of any treatment that was not standard medical treatment and performed in the United States. So, when Mother told me that I should come home and have the surgery where my insurance would pay for it, I was not surprised. It just confirmed that it was God Who would be ordering the circumstances for my recovery.

The next morning the patients had another scheduled worship service, and I had been asked to be prepared to read a scripture. Not sure which scripture to read, I asked one of the patients who had completed the treatment and was leaving the hospital before the service to suggest one. She said her favorite scripture was Psalm 27, so I read it to everyone that day:

> The LORD is my light and my salvation; whom shall I fear? The LORD is the strength of my life; of whom shall I be afraid? When the wicked, even mine enemies and my foes, came upon me to eat up my flesh, they stumbled and fell. Though an host should encamp against me, my heart shall not fear: though war should rise against me, in this will I be confident. One thing have I desired of the LORD, that will I seek after; that I may dwell in the house of the LORD all the days of my life, to behold the beauty of the LORD, and to enquire in his temple. For in the time of trouble he shall hide me in his pavilion: in the secret of his tabernacle shall he hide me; he shall set me up upon a rock.
>
> And now shall mine head be lifted up above mine

enemies round about me: therefore will I offer in his tabernacle sacrifices of joy; I will sing, yea, I will sing praises unto the LORD.
Hear, O LORD, when I cry with my voice: have mercy also upon me, and answer me. When thou saidst, Seek ye my face; my heart said unto thee, Thy face, LORD, will I seek. Hide not thy face far from me; put not thy servant away in anger: thou hast been my help; leave me not, neither forsake me, O God of my salvation. When my father and my mother forsake me, then the LORD will take me up.
Teach me thy way, O LORD, and lead me in a plain path, because of mine enemies. Deliver me not over unto the will of mine enemies: for false witnesses are risen up against me, and such as breathe out cruelty. I had fainted, unless I had believed to see the goodness of the LORD in the land of the living.
Wait on the LORD: be of good courage, and he shall strengthen thine heart: wait, I say, on the LORD."

That Scripture spoke to me in a way that I had never known before. On the very day, when I was searching for provision for a surgery that I needed, the Lord instructed me in the final verse: *"Wait on the LORD: be of good courage, and he shall strengthen thine heart: wait, I say, on the LORD."* It was an instruction to be patient, something I have never been very good at.

I read this entire chapter of Psalm 27 during the service Sunday morning. I don't know if it affected anyone else the way it did me, but I will never forget how God used that friend to lead me to just the right scripture at just the right moment in my life.

On Monday morning, January 29, I was passing one of the treatment lounges when I saw Esther sitting all alone, taking her daily IV treatment. She and her husband had put together that Wednesday evening prayer meeting as well as the Sunday service. Jon played the guitar, which made singing hymns much more enjoyable. As I approached Esther to say hello, she asked: "When will you be having your surgery?"

"Oh, I won't be having surgery," I said.

"Why not?" she asked.

I explained that we didn't have that kind of money. "Well, how much is it?" she asked.

I told her, "Thirteen thousand, nine hundred and fifty dollars."

When she heard that, her arms flew up into the air, the IV tubes dangling, and she exclaimed, "Well, do it, girl! I'll pay for it. I have my checkbook with me."

I must have just stood there dumbfounded by what she was volunteering to do, because the next thing I heard was her saying, "Well! Go! Go! Set it up with the doctor."

With tears in my eyes and feeling more blessed than I had ever felt in my entire life, I raced off to make the arrangements, telling everyone I passed about how God had used Esther to provide for my surgery. Everyone commented how they had never seen anyone so excited about having surgery. Well, this wasn't just any old surgery. I believe God had orchestrated every phase of this operation and that Jon and Esther were willingly used as instruments in the hands of the Lord.

The surgery was scheduled for the next morning at 8. I was so excited about the series of events that had gotten me this far that I had no fear, only complete and total faith that I was going to be cured. I had never experienced such joy! I felt like I was on top of the world!

The last thing I remember before surgery was the anesthesiologist praying with me as he put me to sleep. When I awoke, the first thing I remember was the clock on the wall reading 10:15 a.m.

Then I noticed that on either side of my bed were Jon and Esther, the dear angels the Lord had used to finance my surgery. Esther said they had been supposed to leave the hospital that morning at 8, but they were not about to leave until they knew that I was okay.

She went on to tell me that when they checked out, they were told they still owed for vitamins and supplements the hospital was sending home with them. She asked the receptionist if I could expect to have a bill like that when I checked out, and the receptionist said, "Yes. Everyone is sent home with vitamins." Now, Esther patted my hand and said, "Don't worry about it. We left a check to cover those expenses. If it's more than they need, just keep it."

Jon and Esther are indeed modern-day Good Samaritans, just like the story in Luke 10:27-37. I was basically a stranger to them, and yet they made provision for my immediate need of surgery. Then they saw to it that all my expenses would be taken care of while I was in the hospital and beyond. What an awesome God we serve!

The surgery was a complete success. The doctor was able to remove the tumor, all the inflammatory tissue surrounding it, and do reconstructive surgery—all in a single intervention. Following the surgery, I was required to take a vaccine made from the tumor that had been removed from my body. I took the vaccine orally, once a day for one week, then once a week for five weeks, then once a month for the next seven months. I also took large quantities of vitamins, minerals, Omega 3s and enzymes.

During this time, I continued my diet of seventy percent fresh raw fruits and vegetables, lots of juicing and meals consisting of only thirty percent lean meat, organic rice, beans, nuts and dairy products.

In November of 2007, I had a PET scan, and the results came back clear. There was no sign of cancer in my body! I had won the battle!

I know the Lord is always with me. However, during the years I battled cancer, I felt His presence more than ever before. Paul assured the Philippian believers:

Philippians 4:19
My God shall supply all your needs according to his riches in glory by Christ Jesus.

God, being always true to His Word, did indeed supply all my needs.

I believe God allowed me to get sick in order to strengthen my faith. Now, through this book, I pray that others going through similar health issues will also be encouraged and their faith in God's healing power strengthened. God designed us to be resilient. The psalmist said:

Psalm 139:14
I will praise You, for I am fearfully and wonderfully made ... .

I pray that the information provided in this book will give you the courage and faith in God's healing power to make natural healing your first consideration. Choose to take control of your health. Natural treatments are not the easy way. You have to be involved with your diet and lifestyle on a daily basis. You can't just take a pill and expect to feel better immediately. However, your body will respond to healthy changes you make to your diet and lifestyle, and you will rapidly begin to see a reduction in your symptoms and experience the resilience and vitality God designed you with.

Chapter 2

A Day I Will Never Forget

I know that God has been instrumental throughout my life, using my experiences—both good and bad—to form and perfect me to become someone He can use to do His will. When I was diagnosed with cancer, I learned to put my faith in Him, and during the process, He confirmed that He is the Great Physician. His creative hand is at work in natural healing. But it was a process I would have to follow.

Wednesday January 25, 2006 was a day I will never forget. It was on that evening that I discovered the lump in my breast. Instantly, I got that sickening feeling that I had breast cancer. Richard and I were uninsured at the time, which complicated the matter even further. I knew that we did not have the financial means to seek normal treatments.

After spending a tearful and prayerful sleepless night, I contacted a local physician first thing the next

A Day I Will Never Forget

morning. I was amazed and delighted when he was able to schedule me immediately. Upon examination, he confirmed my suspicions, and said, "The lump appears to be cancerous." He promptly sent me to a local hospital for a mammogram and an ultrasound. The radiologist again confirmed my fears and then sent me back to the physician to schedule an appointment with the surgeon.

The physician explained that I would be asked to sign papers allowing the surgeon to perform whatever type surgery he felt necessary and considered most effective to reduce the risk of the cancer spreading or recurring. The consent form would give the surgeon permission to do a total mastectomy rather than a simple lumpectomy, if he felt that it would reduce my risk of developing breast cancer again in the future.

My instant thought was, "Of course, he'll choose total mastectomy. The cancer can't recur if I don't have a breast." Then, after surgery, I would be required to have chemotherapy and radiation. I felt that the physician was encouraging the most drastic treatment—a total mastectomy—followed by poisonous chemotherapy and radiation. This seemed extreme to me, especially considering the fact that the lump was only the size of the tip of my thumb.

For the next several days, there was a continual gnawing in my stomach, a real hesitation about agreeing to such an extreme process without a second opinion. So, the following Monday morning I called and cancelled the appointment with the surgeon and contacted a specialist for a second opinion. He was supposedly the best in the area, so naturally he was booked up for weeks. After pleading with his nurse, she amazingly worked me in by the end of the week.

Fortunately, Richard and I had the next few days to pray and contact friends and family members for moral support and encouragement. Two of our dearest colleagues and their wives—John and his wife Sharon and Jim and his wife Nellie—volunteered to loan us a total of $25,000 interest free for five years to help with medical expenses. God is so good! He is always with us and knows our every need, even before we do. Jesus Himself said:

Matthew 6:8, AMPC
Your Father knows what you need before you ask Him.

Our prayers were answered. The financial concerns that were facing us had been lifted.

After researching the effects to one's body caused by the standard medical treatment for cancer, my long-standing confidence in the natural and alternative approaches to healing were reinforced. I couldn't even read about the devastating side effects of chemotherapy and radiation without bursting into tears. By the time I visited the surgeon, I was pretty well convinced that I wanted to try an alternative form of treatment

A Day I Will Never Forget

before undergoing extensive, mutilating surgery and subjecting my body to poisonous chemicals. However, I wanted to have a biopsy done to confirm that the lump was indeed cancerous and not just a cyst or some other form of tumor.

The surgeon told me about an insurance program offered by the state of Tennessee for women diagnosed with cancer. What a relief that was! I knew that God had put the check in my spirit that I needed a second opinion, and He used my sister-in-law, Connie, to refer me to a physician who knew of this program. This relieved me of the stress and expense of going through a devastating medical situation without insurance.

The biopsy was performed. Much to my amazement, it was completely painless, perhaps partially because I was on Cloud Nine at the time. Whatever the diagnosis, the medical treatment would be covered, and Richard and I would not have to sell our home to pay for it. Another appointment was made to return in one week to receive the biopsy results.

Before returning for the results, I contacted the office of Dr. Dan Clark, the naturopathic physician under whom I had studied. He had also treated me years before for migraine headaches. I felt confident that he could diagnose the cause of my cancer through bioenergetic testing. This was the way he had diagnosed the cause of my migraines years earlier. I also believed that he would be able to help me develop a natural treatment protocol, to activate my body's natural responses—building up my immune system to detoxify my body, ultimately destroying the cancer cells that were overpowering my system. For sure my migraine headaches had gone away, and I believed my cancer would do the same.

I had suffered with migraine headaches from my early twenties well into my thirties—more than fifteen years. Every month I would start my period and, then, within a day or two, get a migraine headache that lasted for three days. I tried chiropractic treatment, medical treatment and pharmaceutical drugs to relieve the pain, but nothing helped. Prescription drugs numbed the pain, but the headaches continued to come every month like clockwork.

I was introduced to naturopathic medicine and bioenergetic testing one weekend while attending a medical conference. Without asking any health questions, a survey was performed using a probe that checked electrical impulses from the acupuncture points on my fingers and toes. These measurements apparently showed that my liver was toxic. I was told that I was probably having migraine headaches and had irregularity problems. Needless to say, I was amazed at the accuracy of that diagnosis. I had suffered with both of these conditions for years.

More than one physician had told me that nothing could be done about the migraines (with the exception of pain-relieving drugs), and they also insisted, "Infrequent bowel movements are just normal for

A Day I Will Never Forget

some people." I believe I was told that by the same physician who, when I asked him about my mood swings, answered, "All women are bitches, and there is nothing that can be done about it." No wonder I decided to study naturopathic medicine!

I knew that a slow transit time for food through the intestines caused toxic waste to build up, enter the bloodstream, and affect our liver and various other organs of the body. A toxic liver *can* cause migraine headaches. And research has proven that women who have two or fewer bowel movements per week have four times the risk of breast disease (benign or malignant) as women who have one or more bowel movements per day. [1]

The naturopathic recommendation for treatment of my migraines was to take five homeopathic detoxifying remedies three times each day for the next three months. I changed nothing in my diet or lifestyle, just put ten drops of each remedy under my tongue three times each day for the next three months. At the end of the first month, I did get the migraine, right on schedule, but it only lasted one day. That was exciting!

The following month, I again got the migraine right on schedule, but it lasted only one hour. I couldn't believe it! By the third month, I didn't get a migraine

---

1. Constipation and Breast Cancer, *Saturday Evening Post*, April 1982; 2 Physicians, Nicholas L. Petrakis and Eileen B. King, of the University of California, writing in *Lancet*

at all! From that point to this day, I don't get migraine headaches! I had long believed strongly in homeopathy and the natural healing approach to treatment for illness and disease. Now, years later, when confronted with another health issue, the natural, holistic approach was again my choice.

When the biopsy results came back positive, the surgeon recommended that I speak with an oncologist so that he could explain the treatment he recommended. The oncologist told me that, after surgery, I would need to undergo seven weeks of daily radiation treatments followed by eight months of chemotherapy and be on numerous pharmaceutical drugs to reduce the chance of the cancer recurring. All this treatment was required, unless I agreed to a total mastectomy and only if no new cancer cells were detected in my lymph glands.

My medical background taught me that the lymph system is part of our body's protective mechanism. If undisturbed, the lymph system is designed to overcome disease, and this included malignancy. However, this protective system would be significantly damaged and its effectiveness compromised by removal of the nodes.[2]

It is common knowledge today that X-rays are dangerous and too much exposure to them will lead to cancer. Chemotherapy is such a dangerous chemical

---

2. Cameron, Dr. Ewan and Pauling, Dr. Linus. AlkalizeForHealth http://www.alkalizeforhealth.net/rebounder.htm

that it will destroy any skin tissue if comes in contact with. Nurses are strictly warned against letting any of the chemical touch their skin or get on their clothing.

My review of some of the most commonly prescribed breast cancer drugs revealed their terrible side effects. For example, Herceptin can have serious effects, such as heart damage, which may lead to heart failure. It can also affect the lungs, causing breathing problems. Avastin may cause problems with wound healing, which could result in bleeding or infections. Aromasin can cause vision problems, joint pain, headaches, high blood pressure and a whole list of other miseries. The risks of prolonged side effects from the standard medical approach to treatment was overwhelming. I knew that taking the natural treatment approach would activate my body's natural responses, building up my immune system and detoxify my body, all without harsh side effects or the requirement to depend on pharmaceutical drugs for the rest of my life. That sounded so much better to me.

Therefore, on my return visit to the surgeon, I informed him that I had decided to take an alternative approach to treating the cancer and believed God would guide and direct my path to recovery. The surgeon shook his head in disapproval and said he did not agree with my decision. He told me, "The only other patient I had who believed that God would heal her was dead within six months."

My feelings were that I would be a hypocrite if I just ignored all my training in natural healing—everything that I believed in and preached to others—without even giving my body the chance to heal naturally. I knew that radiation and chemotherapy were poisons that would put added strain on my already-weakened immune system, and both have been linked to the development of recurring cancer. Therefore, I walked out of the physician's office that day more determined than ever and feeling empowered and strengthened by my decision to prove the healing power of prayer. I knew that God would give me wisdom and guide and direct my path to healing. My firm belief in the healing power of God Almighty is affirmed by His words:

Exodus 15:26, NKJV
For I am the Lord, who heals you.

My faith was as Abraham's:

Romans 4:19-21, My Paraphrase
His faith did not weaken when he considered the impotence of his own body ... no unbelief or distrust made him waver concerning the promise of God. He grew strong and empowered by faith as he gave praise and glory to God, fully satisfied and assured that He was able and mighty to keep His word and do what He had promised.

A Day I Will Never Forget

I also believe the prolific author, Dr. T.C. Fry, was right when he said, "You cannot poison your body into health with drugs, chemo, or radiation. The holistic approach treats the whole animal, ignites the body's internal healing force and stimulates the body's natural abilities to heal itself. Health can only be achieved with healthful living."[3]

Natural treatment would not be covered by insurance, but thank God our friends were moved to loan us the money we would need to pursue the natural approach to curing the cancer. It seems a shame that insurance companies and our government willingly pay out hundreds of thousands of dollars for medical treatment only when recommended by allopathic (medical) physicians and only for standard treatment. There is a plethora of evidence that natural and holistic methods of treatment are by far safer and frequently more effective. With the cost of cancer treatment increasing year after year and the dangerous side effects of cancer drugs, it seems that our government and insurance companies would insist on offering patients alternative treatments for cancer therapy.

Dr. Julian M. Whitaker says this about the treatment of cancer: "What is lost in the unemotional statistic of 500,000 cancer deaths per year is how those people died. In my opinion, conventional cancer therapy is so toxic and dehumanizing that I fear it far more than I fear death from cancer. We know that conventional

---
3. http://www.alternativehealth.co.nz/cancer/index.htm

therapy doesn't work. If it did, you would not fear cancer any more than you fear pneumonia. It is the utter lack of certainty as to the outcome of conventional treatment that virtually screams for more freedom of choice in the area of cancer therapy. Yet most so-called alternative therapies, regardless of potential or proven benefit, are outlawed, which forces patients to submit to the failures that we know don't work, because there's no other choice."[4]

Here is a story from an anonymous cancer patient that serves as one example of how outrageous cancer treatment costs have become:

> "Every three weeks, always on a Thursday afternoon, I amble on over to the cancer center for my IV treatment. (I also take Cytoxan, a chemo drug that comes in pill form, every day, plus a handful of other pills to help deal with the side effects and fringe benefits of being in cancer treatment—anxiety, high blood pressure, occasional depression, insomnia.)
>
> "The total bill for each treatment session at the cancer center is something north of $20,000. The annual cost of my cancer care is more than $300,000. That's three hundred thousand dollars a year. Almost, $30,000 a month to keep me alive.
>
> "Here's how the costs break down:

---
4. http://www.alternativehealth.co.nz/cancer/index.htm

A Day I Will Never Forget

"My bill from the Seattle Cancer Care Alliance (where I got my treatment until recently) for September 1, 2006, for three drugs—Herceptin, Avastin, and Zometa—was for $20,052.19.

"The cost of the three drugs, listed as "drugs/detail code," was $18,142.92. I asked at the pharmacy, and they told me that they charged me $6,254.95 for one dose of Herceptin, and an amazing $9,496.47 for one dose of Avastin. In addition, SCCA charged me almost $2,000 to give me this one treatment."

On the next page I have included a chart from the National Cancer Institute which shows the rising cost of cancer treatment from 1963 through 2004, an astonishing rise in cost from $1,300,000,000 to an unbelievable $72,100,000,000 in 2004. No wonder our nation's healthcare system is in crisis!

I was not sure what the cost would be to cure cancer naturally, but I did know it would cost considerably less than the standard medical treatment. My philosophy was that it would be better to restore my body to health through natural means. I just didn't believe that poisoning my body with chemotherapy drugs or burning it with radiation was the way back to health.

I so strongly believed this treatment choice was the right one for me and a win-win decision that I now had no fear. I believed what Paul expressed in his letter to the Philippians:

Philippians 1:21

For to me, to live is Christ, and to die is gain.

I knew I would rather trust in God than in man. If, in the process, I was healed, what a wonderful testimony I would have! If I died, I would spend eternity with my heavenly Father! Either way, I could not lose! Here is that chart:

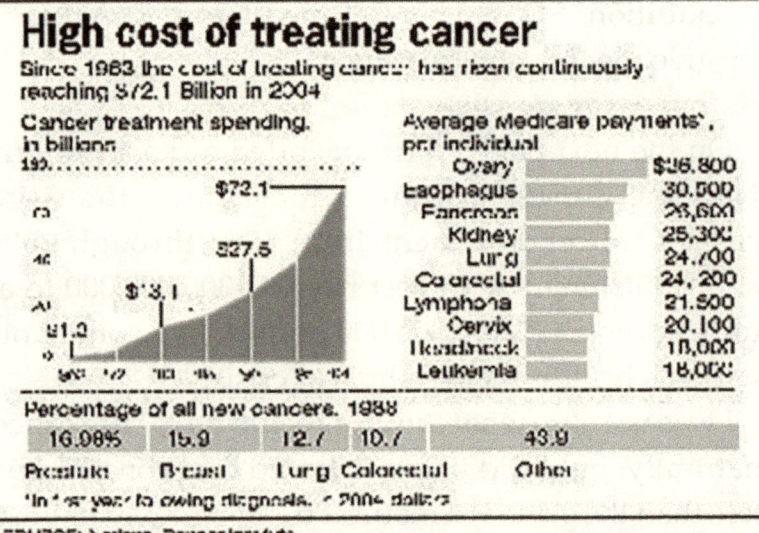

I have purposely laced this book with many encouraging quotes and scripture after scripture assuring us of God's love and compassion. These and many more messages inspired me and strengthened me to continue when no improvement in my condition was obvious.

A Day I Will Never Forget

More than a hundred years ago, Thomas Edison (1847-1931) said, "The doctor of the future will give no medicine, but will interest her or his patients in the care of the human frame, in a proper diet, and in the cause and prevention of disease" and "The doctor of the future will no longer treat the human frame with drugs, but rather will cure and prevent disease with nutrition."[5]

The author, Jethro Kloss, has said, "God, in His infinite wisdom, neglected nothing, and if we would eat our food without trying to improve, change, or refine it, thereby destroying its life-giving elements, it would meet all requirements of the body."[6]

Edison and Kloss knew that disease is caused by the effects of an improper diet and stress and, therefore, can be cured if we use what God has created in its natural form and not exist entirely on foods robbed of their life-giving elements and packed with artificial ingredients, preservatives, food coloring, and other additives.

This is the story about what I did and did not do during the course of the next two years to help restore my body to health and defeat the cancer the natural way. I wrote this book because the Word of God commands us to tell of our blessings and miracles so that others will be encouraged, and their faith will be increased.

Jesus taught us:

---
5. http://www.quotationspage.com/quotes/Thomas_A._Edison/
6. Kloss, Jethro, *Back to Eden*, 1939

Matthew 5:16
> *Let your light so shine before men, that they may see your good works and glorify your Father in heaven.*

Hopefully, through this book, I will help others understand how our bodies are designed and what they require in order to be healed and remain healthy. Putting your faith and trust in God through prayer and praise, lay your cares upon Jesus, do your part to give your body the nutrition it needs to regain health, and I believe you, too, will experience healing miracles. The Scriptures say it so well:

Psalm 139:14
> *I praise you because I am fearfully and wonderfully made; your works are wonderful, I know that full well.*

Even Gautama Buddha said, "The secret of health for both mind and body is not to mourn for the past, not to worry about the future, or not to anticipate troubles, but to live the present moment wisely and earnestly."[7]

---
7. https://sidsavara.com/start-pages/be-present-in-the-moment/ (Accessed 10/18/2019)

Chapter 3

The Role of Healing Prayers

My initial treatment started with intensive prayers for healing and asking God to lead my research and divulge whatever method was necessary to heal my body of cancer. Then I immediately began praising God for my healing and for giving me the opportunity to prove that He was the Great Physician:

Mark 11:24
Therefore I say unto you, What things soever ye desire, when ye pray, believe that ye receive them, and ye shall have them.

Healing prayers are for all those who long for the healing power of our Lord and Savior. These prayers are offered in faith and hope that we might all experience healing of body, mind and spirit in every aspect of our lives.

Our desire for healing, or wholeness, is directly related to our faith in God and to our openness to the love of the Holy Spirit. If we truly believe in God's power to heal and in His deep love for us, God will guide us with His infinite wisdom in every situation and circumstance. As we turn our needs over to God in prayer, healing can and will occur.

We tend to think of healing only in a physical sense, but healing can and does have a much broader significance in our lives. The words *health, healing, holiness* and *wholeness* are all derived from the same root word, *hal*, which means "whole or unhurt." True healing involves not only the physical but also the mental, emotional and spiritual aspects of our lives.

There is no "right" or "best" way to pray for healing. What is most important is not *how* we pray, but only that we pray. When we pray, God is there for us. He is listening to our prayers and touching our lives with His healing and love. His Word declares:

Matthew 7:7
> *Ask, and it shall be given you; seek, and ye shall find; knock, and it shall be opened unto you: For every one that asketh receiveth; and he that seeketh findeth; and to him that knocketh it shall be opened.*

The Role of Healing Prayers

2 Kings 20:5
Thus saith the Lord, the God of David thy father, I have heard thy prayer, I have seen thy tears: behold, I will heal thee.

Mark 9:23
Jesus said unto him, If thou canst believe, all things are possible to him that believeth.

Matthew 8:13
... As thou hast believed, so be it done unto thee.

1 Thessalonians 5:17
Pray without ceasing.

Isaiah 41:10, My Paraphrase
... Do not be afraid, for I am with you; stop being anxious and watchful, for I am your God. I give you strength, I bring you help, I uphold you with my victorious right hand.

ST. FRANCIS' PRAYER

Lord, make me an instrument of Your peace.
Where there is hatred, let me sow love,
Where there is injury, pardon.
Where there is discord, union.
Where there is doubt, faith.
Where there is despair, hope.

Where there is darkness, light.
And where there is sadness, joy.
O Master, grant that I may not so much seek to be consoled, as to console;
to be understood, as to understand;
to be loved, as to love;
for it is in giving that we receive.
It is in pardoning that we are pardoned.
And it is in dying that we are born to eternal life.

As we have seen, the promise of God is:

James 1:5
If any of you lack wisdom, let him ask of God, that giveth to all men liberally, and upbraideth not; and it shall be given him.

I loved God and was believing that I would see His unfailing promises fulfilled in my body.

CHAPTER 4

Treatment Decisions

The treatment method I chose would require a monthly trip to see Dr. Jonathan Clark in Melbourne, Florida. At his clinic, I would be tested using the Computron, a bioenergetic device that checks acupressure points (meridians) throughout the body and gives readings on each organ system. "Because the meridians influence every cell in the body and pass through every organ and organ system, acupuncture (meridians) provides the health practitioners with an accurate and noninvasive means of determining health deficiencies as well as a method of reestablishing balance."[1] Using this technology, one can determine the effectiveness of various nutrients, remedies, vitamins and minerals on balancing and bringing the organ system back into harmony.

---
1. William Michael Cargile, B.S., D.C., F.I.A.C.A., Chairman of Research for the American Association of Acupuncture and Oriental Medicine

I quickly learned several important lessons:

- Vitamins, minerals and other natural substances can be as expensive as pharmaceutical drugs.
- Just because something natural is touted as being helpful for a particular condition does not mean it will work effectively for everyone.
- Combining nutritional supplements can be as dangerous as combining pharmaceutical drugs.
- Taking the wrong combination of supplements also wastes precious time and money.

The technology to check the effectiveness of drugs and natural remedies has been available to the medical profession and recognized as accurate by the Food and Drug Administration for many years. I believe it should be required that this technology be used by every physician, pharmacist, dietician and health food store in the world before they recommend or prescribe anything to their patients. However, our physicians continue to prescribe drugs without knowing what side effects they will have on their patients or if they will even be effective for the condition for which they are being prescribed.

Have you ever heard the saying? "What you don't know won't hurt you." That cannot be further from the truth! What you don't know about staying healthy *CAN* keep you ill or even kill you!

Our physicians should stop "practicing" and experimenting on us and start prescribing only the

Treatment Decisions

supplements and products that will actually help heal us, without causing dangerous side effects. It upsets me when someone tells me their physician has prescribed drug after drug, instructing that they stop taking them if they have any of the dozens of potential side effects that the literature mentions. Patients are mere guinea pigs when it comes to prescription drugs. This haphazard approach to treating illness and disease could be eliminated with technology that has already been proven.

There is an abundance of documented information regarding the limitations and abuse of our modern medical establishment, and this bolstered my decision to take the natural approach to healing. Some medical professionals have been bold enough to speak out concerning the state of our healthcare system and our out-of-control pharmaceutical costs. The United States spends more on healthcare and pharmaceutical drugs than any other nation in the world, and according to Forbes statistics, the United States is not even listed in the top ten healthiest countries.

Research done by Robert I. Bender, M.D., FAAFP, found that from 1960 to 1980, prescription drug sales were fairly steady as a percentage of the U.S. gross domestic product, but from 1980 to 2000, they tripled. According to the Retail Drug Monitor (IMS): "Global pharmaceutical sales through retail pharmacies increased 5% in just one year between November 2005 and November 2006, standing now at $386.23 billion per year."[2]

In 2002, the combined profits for the ten drug companies on the Fortune 500 list was $35.9 billion. All the other 490 businesses put together brought in only $33.7 billion. This means that the top ten drug companies made more profit than all the other Fortune 500 companies put together.[3]

According to Dr. Joseph Michael Mercola, a well known alternative medicine proponent, America has the best system in the entire world for treating acute surgical emergencies. However, beyond that, the system is an unmitigated failure at treating chronic illness.[4]

When compared to other developed countries, the United States falls behind in terms of life expectancy. It is not among the top ten in the world and, in fact, is among those countries of the world at the lower end of the economic scale. The U.S. life expectancy level is close to that of Cuba.[5]

According to the Journal of the American Medical Association (JAMA), prescription drugs are now the fourth leading medical cause of death in the U.S. and Canada, behind only cancer, heart disease and stroke, which "are facilitated largely by physician

---

2. Heath Ledger Legacy: Prescription Drugs a Silent Killer. September 19, 2008
3. Angell, Marcia. Excess in the pharmaceutical industry. CMAJ, December 7, 2004
4. Dr. Mercola. U.S. Health System, Most Expensive in the World, January 2, 2008
5. Epidemiology And Today's Deadliest Diseases. http://www.videojug.com/interview/epidemiology-and-todays-deadliest-diseases-2

Treatment Decisions

ignorance of foundational concepts of nutritional physiology."[6]

According to William J. Kassler, past President of the AMSA, "the teaching of nutrition in most U.S. medical schools is inadequate. Education has traditionally focused on the principles of acute episodic health-care delivery, overlooking the concepts and application of nutrition and preventive medicine. Nutrition is not well taught, if taught at all, in most medical schools."[7]

A recent study performed by the University of North Carolina and entitled "Nutrition Education in U.S. Medical Schools" revealed that almost all schools now require exposure to the subject of nutrition. However, only about a quarter offer the recommended twenty-five hours of instruction and only a quarter of the schools managed to have a single course dedicated to the topic.[8]

As noted, because American medical doctors continue to focus on acute episodic health-care delivery and overlook the concepts and application of nutrition and preventive medicine, the physical health of Americans continues to deteriorate, with increasing numbers of chronically ill people with no hope of recovery and a life spent in a suspended state of ill

---

6. The Leading Cause of Death in U.S. Prescription Drugs. 12/9/09 Drug Alert. http://www.the7thfire.com/health_and_nutrition/Prescription_drugs_deaths.htm.
7. Kassler, William J., AMSA National President, Testimony of the American Medical Student Association: Nutrition Education in the Undergraduate Medical Curriculum, page 121, January 14, 1985
8. DiNapoli, Marianne, Nutrition – a gap in medical education, September 16, 2010

health and dependence on pharmaceutical drugs. This empties their pocketbooks and destroys any hope of restoration.

Each year, prescription drugs cause serious reactions and permanent disability for over 2.2 million people. More people are killed by prescription drugs each year than were killed in the entire Vietnam War.[9]

An article by Drs. Holland and DeGruy suggests that as many as ten percent of hospital admissions may be attributable to prescription drug-induced disorders.[10]

Two facts many people do not realize are:

1. Prescription drugs can be as dangerous as street drugs.
2. The vast majority of drugs—more than 90 percent—only work in 30% to 50% of the people.

According to Dr. Allen Roses, the Worldwide Vice President of GlaxoSmithKline, "Cancer drugs only work 25% of the time, Alzheimer's drugs work 30% of the time, and many others only 50% of the time."[11]

On average, fifty-one percent of drugs approved by the Food and Drug Administration (FDA) have serious

---

9. Bender, Robert I, M.D., FAAFP. The Pharmaceutical "Business with Disease" September 29, 2008
10. Holland and DeGruy. American Academy of Family Physicians. June
11. Connor, Steve. Glaxo Chief: Our Drugs Do Not Work on Most Patients, Common Dreams, December 8, 2003

Treatment Decisions

adverse side effects that have not been not detected prior to their approval for public use. This is why pharmaceuticals actually contribute to hospitalization, permanent disabilities, disease, illness and death.

The "Father of Medicine," Hippocrates, is well-known for saying, "as far as disease, help or at least do no harm." Unfortunately, it appears that the pharmaceutical industry is more focused on making a profit than on curing disease.[12]

It is notable that the pharmaceutical industry spends more than twice as much on advertising and administration than it spends on research. Since 1990, prescription drug rates have gone up 500%. Advertisements on television, radio and in national publications are constantly promoting everything from drugs for serious to mild ailments. This encourages people to diagnose their own condition and request drugs from their physician.

Peter R. Breggin, M.D., a former consultant at the National Institute of Mental Health and author of the book *Medical Madness*," stated, "The population of North America is one of the most heavily medicated in the world," and "the profitable pharmaceutical industry has created a disturbingly legal drug-addicted society."[13] If I had chosen the standard medical treatment and survived, I would have always wondered if

---

12. Cohen, Jay, M.D. Campaign for Truth, The Case Against the Drug Companies. February 2002
13. Breggin, Peter R., MD. *Medical Madness*. July 2008

I had survived not *because of* the drugs and surgery but *in spite of* them.

As I searched for natural cures for cancer, these promises from God's Word encouraged me to continue seeking:

James 1:5
If any of you lack wisdom, let him ask of God, that giveth to all men liberally, and upbraideth not; and it shall be given him.

Matthew 7:7
Ask, and it shall be given you; seek, and ye shall find; knock, and it shall be opened unto you.

During my research, I found over three hundred proven cures for cancer described in-depth, along with a plethora of testimonials from common people who had opted out of standard medical treatments and been healed of, not only cancer, but a multitude of other illnesses as well. My prayer was that God would guide me to what my body needed in order to be restored to health, and that He would give me the faith to stand firm in His healing power. I also prayed for wisdom for the Naturopathic physician treating me.

On my first visit to this man, he warned me to stay away from negative people. It is crucial that one's mind and spirit remain positive and uplifted. We must heed the apostle Paul's instructions:

Treatment Decisions

Philippians 4:8

Finally, brethren, whatsoever things are true, whatsoever things are honest, whatsoever things are just, whatsoever things are pure, whatsoever things are lovely, whatsoever things are of good report; if there be any virtue, and if there be any praise, think on these things.

A positive mental attitude and faith in the healing power of God empowers your body and stimulates the healing process.

Philippians 4:7

And the peace of God, which passeth all understanding, shall keep your hearts and minds through Christ Jesus.

It worked for me.

CHAPTER 5

Overcoming the Skepticism of Many

The one thing I was not prepared for was the skepticism many had about the treatment option I chose. When I was warned by my Naturopathic physician to stay away from negative people, I did not realize that it would be some of those closest to me who would not agree with this decision. The Bible instructs us:

2 Corinthians 6:14-15
Do not be unequally yoked together with unbelievers ... what part has a believer with an unbeliever?

To stand firm in my belief in God's healing power, it was essential to avoid those whose faith was inconsistent with my own. For all their well-intended concern, the roughest part of the next two years of my life was by far the agony I felt because of the negative opinions of others and their disbelief in what I

Overcoming the Skepticism of Many

was doing. They believed I had lost my mind and was committing suicide because I opted out of what the so-called medical professionals told me was my only option.

Some were willing to help in any way possible when they first heard of my diagnosis. Offering to stay with me, take me to the doctor's office, clean my house or prepare meals for me—whatever I needed during the devastating treatment. However, when I told them I was going to put my faith in God and trust that everything I had learned in my medical training was factual, their concern turned to fear and skepticism.

To some, my education seemed to be irrelevant. It reminded me of the story in Mark:

Mark 6:4, NKJV
But Jesus said to them, "A prophet is not without honor except in his own country, among his own relatives, and in his own house."

I realized there was nothing I could say to give others confidence in my decision. I prayed daily as the apostle Paul had:

Philippians 4:7
And the peace of God, which passeth all understanding, shall keep your hearts and minds through Christ Jesus.

Only God could give these skeptics peace because they could not understand my faith or my commitment to natural healing.

I had many conversations with God about how it was going to look if I didn't recover from this illness. I had announced to the world that my faith and trust were in His miraculous healing power and my belief that He designed our bodies to heal themselves of disease if given the proper nutrition.

I did everything within my power to restore my body to health and remained focused and confident, reciting constantly: I am healed in the name of Jesus. Cancer has no hold on me.

The one family member who actually encouraged my decision to battle the cancer through natural means as opposed to the standard medical approach was Aunt Nancy, my dad's youngest sister. She had lost her husband a few years earlier, after a long and difficult struggle with cancer. They had followed the doctor's recommendations to the letter—suffering through countless hours of chemotherapy, radiation and other treatments that destroyed my uncle's quality of life and, in the end, only prolonged his agony.

My family and I had always been very close. Now, however, we were at odds over my choice to take control of my own health and, in essence, my own life. It was those who believed in the healing power of prayer and our Lord and Savior's promises who were my strength during this difficult struggle:

Overcoming the Skepticism of Many

Mark 3:35, AMPC
For whoever does the things God wills is My brother and sister and mother!

I made a point of telling everyone I met, any time I was out shopping or just walking, that I was battling breast cancer naturally, with prayer and diet. It seemed a good opportunity to minister to others. Everyone always said: "Good luck! We will pray for you." One day, I mentioned to someone that everyone who didn't know me very well was rooting for me, while my family thought I was crazy. Their response was a revelation. They said: "That's because we don't love you?" I finally realized that my family wasn't against me; they just didn't understand and were afraid for me!

In hindsight, I realize that in many ways the skepticism and lack of faith in natural healing of some of those very close to me had actually forced me to think and speak positively at all times. I knew if I ever said anything negative they would be even more concerned. Therefore, I always said I was doing well! Feeling great! I had to step out of the limitations of my childhood teachings and take the Word of God literally, believing the promise of Hebrews 13:8:

Jesus Christ the same yesterday, and to day, and for ever.

My life depended on God working miraculously, and He did!

CHAPTER 6

What I Did and Why I Did It

My daily routine became extremely regimented. In order to focus totally on getting well, I gave up my job. I actually made a checklist to ensure that I didn't forget any part of the required program throughout the day.

Following is a list of the nutritional items I took daily. The rest and exercise protocol I designed from my extensive research will be covered in a following section. Each nutritional item is listed with a brief description of its content, if applicable, and an explanation of its importance in the overall program. In the following sections, I will elaborate on what I feel are the most important topics and the effect each has on one's body in the healing process.

A quote from a well-known source helped to confirm to me that my decision to go natural was the right one: "As a retired physician, I can honestly say

What I Did and Why I Did It

that unless you are in a serious accident, YOUR BEST CHANCE OF LIVING TO A RIPE OLD AGE IS TO AVOID DOCTORS AND HOSPITALS AND LEARN NUTRITION, HERBAL MEDICINE AND OTHER FORMS OF NATURAL MEDICINE. Almost all drugs are toxic and are designed only to treat symptoms and not to cure anyone. Most surgery is unnecessary. In short, our mainstream medical system is hopelessly inept and/or corrupt. THE TREATMENT OF DEGENERATIVE DISEASES AND CANCER IS A NATIONAL SCANDAL. The sooner you learn this, the better off you will be."[14]

My Daily Regimen

- First thing each morning, prepare eight ounces of warm, purified water with the juice from half of a freshly-squeezed lemon. Add to this mix a generous shake of cayenne pepper. This helps to balance the bodies pH level. Drink this before taking anything else.
- Prepare vegetable juice for the day. Raw vegetable juice provides essential nutrients and enzymes and keeps the body pH balanced.
- Prepare green tea. I would drink up to six cups of it each day. Green Tea Polyphenols (GTP), particularly EGCG or EGCg (epigallocatechin gallate) not only inhibit an enzyme required for cancer cell growth, but also kill cancer cells with

---

14. Greenberg, Dr. Allen, Prevention, 12/24/2002

no ill effect on healthy cells.[15] Researchers from the University of Kansas determined that EGCG is twice as powerful as resveratrol, which itself is known to kill cancer cells.[2]

- Herbs, such as fresh parsley, cilantro and garlic, were added to my vegetable juice and daily meals. Hebrews 6:7: *"For the soil which has drunk the rain that repeatedly falls upon it and produces vegetation useful to those for whose benefit it is cultivated partakes of a blessing from God"* (AMPC).
- A half-hour after drinking the lemon water, take four ounces of freshly-juiced wheat grass or alfalfa sprouts. This stimulates the balancing of the neuro-endocrine system and activates T and B cells.
- Practice rebounding for ten minutes, three to four times each day. Rebounding on a mini-trampoline improves breathing patterns, stimulates lymphatic drainage and improves cellular balance.
- Take Wobenzyme forty-five minutes before each meal. Enzymes taken before meals work at the cellular level to improve metabolism.
- Do stretching and breathing exercises and walk forty-five minutes. This improves lymph drainage and increases breathing, which stimulates oxygen intake, thereby reducing muscle tension and mental stress.

---
15. Purdue University, cancertutorial.com 2, University of Kansas study, 1997

What I Did and Why I Did It

- Drink eight ounces of purified water. Hydration is vitally important to detoxification and proper organ function.
- Brush dry skin. This cleans the skin and circulates and cleanses the lymph system, aiding in the elimination process. Use a natural brush on all areas of the skin except the face and any other sensitive areas. Use long brush strokes, moving toward the heart prior to a shower or bath. (Both the brush and the skin should be dry when this brushing is performed.)
- For breakfast, eat organic oatmeal or fruit with nuts, organic naturally-sweetened yogurt or a veggie omelet.
- Consume eight to sixteen ounces of goat's milk. This is one of the best food medicines for rebuilding the brain, nervous system and mental faculties. It also works to regenerate the cells of the body.
- Take all vitamins that need to be taken with food (multi-vitamins, multi-minerals, omega-3s, Hepasil DTX).
- Take homeopathic remedies one hour after meals. This aids detoxification.
- Do more rebounding. Doing this for ten minutes three or four times a day aids in lymph drainage.
- Drink eight to sixteen ounces of vegetable juice. This provides digestive enzymes and nutrition and balances pH.

- Take Wobenzyme forty-five minutes before lunch for cell metabolism.
- For lunch, have a salad, a veggie wrap or some homemade vegetable broth soup.
- Drink four ounces of Aloe Vera juice. This helps activate white blood cells and promotes the growth of non-cancerous cells. The National Cancer Institute has included Aloe Vera in its recommendations for increased testing because of its apparent cancer-fighting properties. Leviticus 17:11 says: *"For the life of the flesh is in the blood ... ."*
- Again, take vitamins that need to be taken with food.
- Do more breathing exercises and walking outdoors for one hour. Walking improves breathing patterns, stimulates lymphatic drainage and improves cellular balance. The best time to receive adequate sun exposure is between 11:00 a.m. and 2:00 p.m. It is recommended that you get at least ten minutes of direct exposure on your arms and face at least three times a week. This will ensure that you maintain proper vitamin D levels.
- Drink eight ounces of water to maintain hydration.
- Take homeopathic remedies one hour after meals for detoxification.
- Drink eight to sixteen ounces of vegetable juice for enzymes, nutrition and balanced pH.
- Take one ounce of flaxseed oil and four ounces of cottage cheese. Dr. Johanna Budwig's cancer diet

What I Did and Why I Did It

treats patients with a mixture of flax seed oil and quark (a type of cottage cheese). The omega-3 essential oil available from flax oil and ground flax seed is a proven cancer fighter and is also required for proper kidney function.
- Rest and do Christian meditation for one hour between 3 and 5 p.m.
- Drink eight ounces of water to maintain proper hydration.
- Take Wobenzyme forty-five minutes before dinner for cell metabolism.
- For dinner, eat fish or lean meat, whole grain rice and fresh, raw vegetables and herbs. Exodus 12:8 states: *"And they shall eat the flesh in that night, roast with fire, and unleavened bread; and with bitter herbs they shall eat it."* Cold-water or ocean fish contain docosahexanoic acid (DHA), an omega-3 fatty acid which has been shown to reduce the size of tumors.
- As before, take all vitamins that need to be taken with food.
- Take your homeopathic remedies one hour after meals for detoxification.
- Do your breathing exercise and rebounding ten minutes for lymph drainage.
- Take one ounce of flaxseed oil and four ounces of cottage cheese, Dr. Budwig's cancer-cure remedy. Flaxseed oil is rich in omega-3s.
- Sleep at least eight hours, preferably between 9 p.m. and 6 a.m.

Homeopathic Remedies

I took each of the following items at some time during my treatment. However, my nutrition was adjusted as my condition improved:

- **Mammary plex**—stimulates normal mammary function and drainage of breast lymphatics
- **Metalogin**—for heavy metal detoxification, such as from dental amalgam and other metals
- **Inflammation**—reduces inflammation and swelling
- **Systemic Detox**—stimulation of the lymph and spleen, liver and blood
- **Additox**—an insecticide detoxifier, it stimulates release of insecticides into the lymphatics

Botanical Herbs

Romans 14:2

For one believeth that he may eat all things: another, who is weak, eateth herbs.

- **Artemesioplex**—contains wormwood which has a cleansing effect on the stomach, liver and intestine
- **Cilantro**—proven to help combat cancer, it contains caffeic acid and chlorogenic acid antioxidants—two acids that trap free radicals. Eating

just a teaspoon of fresh cilantro every day cuts the risk of cancer.[16]
- **Gerplex II**—cleanses the lymphatic glands and purifies the blood
- **Vermaplex**—fortifies the colon and encourages parasite expulsion
- **Scrofularoplex**—stimulates lymphatic drainage of glandular swelling, congestion in chronic swollen lymph nodes and tenderness in the breast
- **Burdock**—includes chelidonium, containing ten alkaloids which retard tumor growth and a recently identified chemical (arctigenin) which acts as an inhibitor of tumor growth[17]
- **Trifoloplex**—stimulates drainage of breast lymphatics and spleen and is also a lymphatic cleanser and endocrine balancer

Drainage

- **Lymph III**—helps drain enlarged lymph glands, reduces exhaustion and emaciation
- **Hydrate I**—helps with water absorption
- **Liver Tonic III**—stimulates liver detoxification from chemical toxicity
- **Nutritional Support**—supplements provide macro- and micronutrients to aid immune system and metabolic function

---

16. Whatley, T., *Hydrogen Sulf 3X The Undeniable Benefits of Cilantro,* Whitney Worden, December 29, 2008
17. *Natural Cancer Treatment.* 10/14/2008

- **HypoScorbate**—vitamin C has been found to be beneficial for strengthening the immune system and to aid with stress, depression and cancer prevention
- **Natura 401-601**—stimulates lymph drainage
- **Selenium EC**—a component in antioxidant enzymes, it helps prevent DNA damage, boosts immune function, inhibits the growth of blood vessels upon which tumors are dependent and induces cancer cells to self-destruct. Germanium is a trace element (mineral) which promotes cell oxygen absorption.
- **Bio Mer Detox**—a heavy metal detoxification product which helps remove mercury from the body
- **CoQ10**—plays a key role in producing energy in the mitochondria, the part of a cell responsible for the production of energy in the form of ATP
- **Mega Antioxidants**—antioxidants act as "free radical scavengers," preventing or repairing the damage done by free radicals
- **Hepasil DTX**—stimulates detox of the liver
- **Bio Green**—aids the elimination of body wastes and toxins, providing protection from harmful environmental pollution. It also aids in proper cellular metabolism and improved resistance to stress, is a memory enhancer and increases energy levels.
- **Chlorella**—contains vitamin C and carotenoids, antioxidant compounds that block the action of

What I Did and Why I Did It

free radicals, activated oxygen molecules that can damage cells. Chlorella also contains high concentrations of B-complex vitamins. It strengthens the immune system and increases the level of albumin in the body, protecting against diseases such as cancer through its ability to cleanse the body of toxins and heavy metals.
- **Spirulina**—is richly supplied with the blue pigment phycocyanim, an antigen shown to inhibit cancercolony formation
- **Sea Silver**—contains vitamins, minerals, macro-minerals, trace minerals, phytonutrients and all the essential amino acids
- **Waiora Natural Cellular Defense**—natural volcanic minerals, these work at the cellular level, trapping heavy metals and toxins. Because they are negatively-charged minerals, they act as a magnet, drawing toxins—capturing and removing them from the body.[18]

Foods and Their Health Benefits

The following chart is an easy reference guide to the health benefits of many common foods. It was e-mailed to me by my dear friend, Antoinette Sequeira, with instructions to send it to everyone I knew. I can think of no better way to share this helpful and informative list

---
18. Product information provided by BIOActive Nutritional, Inc. & Better Health & Wellness Center

than by including it in this book. Thank you to whoever compiled this wonderful information:

- <u>APPLES</u>: Protect your heart, prevent constipation, block diarrhea, improve lung capacity, and cushion joints
- <u>APRICOTS</u>: Combat cancer, control blood pressure, save your eyesight, shield against Alzheimer's and slow the aging process
- <u>ARTICHOKES</u>: Aid digestion, lower cholesterol, protect your heart, stabilize blood sugar and guard against liver disease
- <u>AVOCADOS</u>: Battle diabetes, lower cholesterol, help stop strokes, control blood pressure and smooth the skin
- <u>BANANAS</u>: Protect your heart, quiet coughs, strengthen bones, control blood pressure and block diarrhea
- <u>BEANS</u>: Prevent constipation, help hemorrhoids, lower cholesterol, combat cancer and stabilize blood sugar
- <u>BEETS</u>: Control blood pressure, combat cancer, strengthen bones, protect your heart and aid weight loss
- <u>BLUEBERRIES</u>: Combat cancer, protect your heart, stabilize blood sugar, boost memory and prevent constipation
- <u>BROCCOLI</u>: Strengthens bones, saves eyesight, combats cancer, protects your heart and controls blood pressure
- <u>CABBAGE</u>: Combats cancer, prevents constipation, promotes weight loss, protects your heart and helps hemorrhoids
- <u>CANTALOUPE</u>: Saves eyesight, controls blood pressure, lowers cholesterol, combats cancer and supports your immune system
- <u>CARROTS</u>: Save eyesight, protect your heart, prevent constipation, combat cancer and promote weight loss

What I Did and Why I Did It

- <u>CAULIFLOWER</u>: Protects against prostate cancer, combats breast cancer, strengthens bones, banishes bruises and guards against heart disease
- <u>CHERRIES</u>: Protect your heart, combat cancer, end insomnia, slow the aging process and shield against Alzheimer's
- <u>CHESTNUTS</u>: Promote weight loss, protect your heart, lower cholesterol, combat cancer and control blood pressure
- <u>CHILI PEPPERS</u>: Aid digestion, soothe sore throat, clear sinuses, combat cancer and boost the immune system
- <u>FIGS</u>: Promote weight loss, help stop strokes, lower cholesterol, combat cancer and control blood pressure
- <u>FISH</u> (Cold-Water Ocean): Lowers blood pressure and blood triglycerides, boosts memory, lowers the risk of Alzheimer's and depression, provides omega-3 fatty acids that protect your heart, reduces inflammation in rheumatoid arthritis, gout and psoriasis, supports the immune system and lowers the risk of cancer
- <u>FLAX</u>: Aids digestion, battles diabetes, protects your heart, improves mental health and boosts the immune system
- <u>GARLIC</u>: Lowers cholesterol, controls blood pressure, combats cancer, kills bacteria and fights fungus
- <u>GRAPEFRUIT</u>: Protects against heart attacks, promotes weight loss, helps stop strokes, combats prostate cancer and lowers cholesterol
- <u>GRAPES</u>: Save eyesight, conquer kidney stones, combat cancer, enhance blood flow, and protect your heart
- <u>GREEN TEA</u>: Combats cancer, protects your heart, helps stop strokes, promotes weight loss and kills bacteria
- <u>HONEY</u>: Heals wounds, aids digestion, guards against ulcers, increases energy and fights allergies

- **LEMONS**: Combat cancer, protect your heart, control blood pressure, smooth the skin and stop scurvy
- **LIMES**: Combat cancer, protect your heart, control blood pressure, smooth the skin and stop scurvy
- **MANGOES**: Combat cancer, boost memory, regulate the thyroid, aid digestion and shield against Alzheimer's
- **MUSHROOMS**: Control blood pressure, lower cholesterol, kill bacteria, combat cancer and strengthen bones
- **OATS**: Lower cholesterol, combat cancer, battle diabetes, prevent constipation and smooth the skin
- **OLIVE OIL**: Protects your heart, promotes weight loss, combats cancer, battles diabetes and smooths the skin
- **ONIONS**: Reduce the risk of heart attack, combat cancer, kill bacteria, lower cholesterol and fight fungus
- **ORANGES**: Support the immune systems, combat cancer (anti-tumor, anti-inflammatory), protect your heart, strengthen respiration and have blood clot inhibiting properties
- **PEACHES**: Prevent constipation, combat cancer, help stop strokes, aid digestion and help relieve hemorrhoids
- **PEANUTS**: Protect against heart disease, promote weight loss, combat prostate cancer, lower cholesterol and aggravate diverticulitis
- **PINEAPPLE**: Strengthens bones, relieves colds, aids digestion, dissolves warts and blocks diarrhea
- **PRUNES**: Slow the aging process, prevent constipation, boost memory, lower cholesterol and protect against heart disease

What I Did and Why I Did It

- **RICE:** Protects your heart, battles diabetes, conquers kidney stones, combats cancer and helps stop strokes
- **STRAWBERRIES:** Combat cancer, protect your heart, boost memory, calm stress and protect cells from free radicals
- **SWEET POTATOES:** Save your eyesight, lift mood, combat cancer, strengthen bones, regulate blood sugar and lower insulin resistance
- **TOMATOES:** Protect the prostate, combat cancer, lower cholesterol, protect your heart and contain Lycopene, a powerful antioxidant
- **WALNUTS:** Lower cholesterol, combat cancer, boost memory, lift mood and protect against heart disease
- **WATER:** Promotes weight loss, combats cancer, conquers kidney stones, smooths the skin and prevents constipation
- **WATERMELON:** Protects the prostate, promotes weight loss, lowers cholesterol, helps stop strokes and controls blood pressure
- **WHEAT GERM:** Combats colon cancer, prevents constipation, lowers cholesterol, helps stop strokes and improves digestion
- **WHEAT BRAN:** Combats colon cancer, prevents constipation, lowers cholesterol, helps stop strokes and improves digestion
- **YOGURT:** Guards against ulcers, strengthens bones, lowers cholesterol, supports the immune systems and aids digestion

It was a combination of all of these important elements that strengthened my body and gave it the ability to heal itself.

> **YE SHALL WALK IN ALL THE WAYS WHICH THE LORD YOUR GOD HATH COMMANDED YOU, THAT YE MAY LIVE, AND THAT IT MAY BE WELL WITH YOU, AND THAT YE MAY PROLONG YOUR DAYS IN THE LAND WHICH YE SHALL POSSESS.**
>
> Deuteronomy 5:33

Chapter 7

Understanding Your Body

I believe that the more a person understands about how their body works the more inclined they will be to make the healthy choices necessary to enhance both the quantity and quality of their life! It has been said, "The greatest wealth is health!" What good is all the money in the world if a person is incapable of enjoying it in good health?

I once heard a comedian say: "If I had known I was going to live so long, I would have taken better care of myself." Of course, that joke aroused a great deal of laughter. In reality, that sentiment needs to be taken very seriously. We only get one life and one body to live out that life! If we abuse that body, we will suffer in our lifetime.

The Bible tells us:

1 Corinthians 6:19-20

Know ye not that your body is the temple of the Holy Ghost which is in you, which ye have of God, and ye are not your own? For you were bought at a price: therefore glorify God in your body, and in your spirit, which are God's.

We are the caretakers of the temple of the Holy Ghost, and in that capacity, we are required to live wise and healthy lives. If we take our guidance from the Word of God for our mental, physical and spiritual living, we will indeed enjoy long and healthy lives.

Ephesians 6:3

That it may be well with thee, and thou mayest live long on the earth.

We must not, however, expect that we will live forever. Our goal should be to remain healthy as long as we are alive. The Word of God specifically states in the following beautiful verses of Ecclesiastes that there is an appointed time for everything, and that each of us has *"a time to die"*:

Ecclesiastes 3:1-8, NIV

There is a time for everything, and a season for every activity under heaven:
a time to be born and a time to die,
a time to plant and a time to uproot,

Understanding Your Body

a time to kill and a time to heal,
a time to tear down and a time to build,
a time to weep and a time to laugh,
a time to mourn and a time to dance,
a time to scatter stones and a time to gather them,
a time to embrace and a time to refrain,
a time to search and a time to give up,
a time to keep and a time to throw away,
a time to tear and a time to mend,
a time to be silent and a time to speak,
a time to love and a time to hate,
a time for war and a time for peace.

Genesis tells us the number of years God intended for us to live on this earth:

Genesis 6:3, NLT
My Spirit will not put up with humans for such a long time, for they are only mortal flesh. In the future, their normal lifespan will be no more than 120 years.

I cannot recall too many times that I have heard of anyone living to be that old. Maybe that is because we are not following the instructions given throughout the Word of God on how to live a long and healthy life.

By misunderstanding that disease processes such as diarrhea, fever and inflammation are not only natural but necessary attempts by the body to regain optimum health, modern medicine frequently attempts to suppress these adaptive and eliminative processes with drugs and other invasive treatments. This may create deeper, more difficult problems, by interfering with the body's self-healing mechanisms.

My goal is to help you become aware of how your body systems function, how to recognize and treat symptoms which are your body's attempt to correct imbalances and disharmony and what you can do to restore and maintain your health naturally.

We are largely in control of how we feel and how we age, as well as how much pain or suffering we will endure in our later life. In other words, our lifestyle today will affect and determine our health or lack thereof in our retirement years.

Deuteronomy 5:33
> *Ye shall walk in all the ways which the LORD your God hath commanded you, that ye may live, and that it may be well with you, and that ye may prolong your days in the land which ye shall possess.*

Micah 6:8
> *... And what doth the LORD require of thee, but to do justly, and to love mercy, and to walk humbly with thy God?*

While doing research on how to cure my body of cancer naturally, I came across biblical principles in modern-day references over and over again. Such evidence encouraged me and helped strengthen my resolve. The Bible has the answers for staying healthy, and they were written down more then two thousand years ago! As Hebrews declares:

Hebrews 13:8
Jesus Christ the same yesterday, and to day, and for ever.

The Word of God is timeless, and it speaks to every aspect of our lives.

The following sections will discuss modern-day scientific findings concerning treatments and cures that God provided when He created the world. Everything He created was *"good."* He filled the world with all we would ever need to live long and healthy lives. However, when sin came into the world, along with it came sickness, disease and, inevitably, physical death.

Still, our loving heavenly Father did not abandon us to this fate:

John 3:16
For God so loved the world, that he gave his only begotten Son, that whosoever believeth in him should not perish, but have everlasting life.

Our Lord and Savior, Jesus Christ, gave Himself for us:

Galatians 1:4

Who gave himself for our sins, that he might deliver us from this present evil world, according to the will of God and our Father.

While Jesus walked the earth, He performed many healing miracles, and, before He left, He told us to do likewise:

John 14:12-14

Verily, verily, I say unto you, He that believeth on me, the works that I do shall he do also; and greater works than these shall he do; because I go unto my Father. And whatsoever ye shall ask in my name, that will I do, that the Father may be glorified in the Son. If ye shall ask any thing in my name, I will do it.

God has said:

Exodus 15:26

If thou wilt diligently hearken to the voice of the LORD thy God, and wilt do that which is right in his sight, and wilt give ear to his commandments, and keep all his statutes, I will put none of these diseases upon thee, which I have brought upon the Egyptians: for I am the LORD that healeth thee.

Therefore, if you are ill, first seek the Lord. The story of Asa warns about only seeking help from physicians:

Understanding Your Body

2 Chronicles 16:12-13, NIV

> *In the thirty-ninth year of his reign Asa was afflicted with a disease in his feet. Though his disease was severe, even in his illness he did not seek help from the LORD, but only from the physicians. Then in the forty-first year of his reign Asa died and rested with his fathers.*

Put your faith in the healing power of God and do not rely solely on physicians.

If and when physicians give you no hope, remember the story of Mark 5:25-29:

> *And a certain woman, which had an issue of blood twelve years, and had suffered many things of many physicians, and had spent all that she had, and was nothing bettered, but rather grew worse, when she had heard of Jesus, came in the press behind, and touched his garment. For she said, If I may touch but his clothes, I shall be whole. And straightway the fountain of her blood was dried up; and she felt in her body that she was healed of that plague.*

This woman's faith was rooted in her understanding of the Word of God from Malachi 4:2:

> *But unto you that fear my name shall the Sun of righteousness arise with healing in his wings.*

This word *"wings"* has been interpreted as "covering" or "garment." Her faith was such that if she only touched the hem of Jesus' garment she would be healed, just as the Scripture said.

Hebrews tells us that we will be rewarded if we are faithful and diligently search the Scriptures for answers:

Hebrews 11:6
He is a rewarder of them that diligently seek him.

John recorded:

John 1:14
And the Word [Jesus] was made flesh.

The psalmist wrote:

Psalm 107:20
He sent he word, and healed them.

In writing to the Church at Philippi, as we noted in an earlier chapter, Paul said:

Philippians 4:8
Finally, brethren, whatsoever things are true, whatsoever things are honest, whatsoever things are just, whatsoever things are pure, whatsoever things are

Understanding Your Body

lovely, whatsoever things are of good report; if there be any virtue, and if there be any praise, think on these things.

Our God has all the answers we need.

> **I THINK MYSELF HAPPY.**
> Acts 26:2

Chapter 8

The Role of Our Mental Attitude in Healing

The wise king Solomon wrote:

Proverbs 18:14, AMPC
The strong spirit of a man sustains him in bodily pain or trouble, but a weak and broken spirit who can raise up or bear?

Ecclesiastes 3:12-13, NIV
I know that there is nothing better for people than to be happy and to do good while they live. That each of them may eat and drink, and find satisfaction in all their toil—this is the gift of God.

Negative emotions and thoughts produce a destructive cycle of physical events that cause the breakdown of health and vitality, and this can eventually lead to the development of disease. It has been proven that emotions, such as stress, anger, anxiety or resentment, cause the body to react in an unhealthy way. Our reaction to these emotions can decrease the oxygen level in our cells and increase our body's acidity, thereby reducing our body's ability to fight disease. By releasing negative emotions, one can improve their health and even eliminate disease!

A positive mental attitude affects every aspect of our life—emotional, mental and spiritual. If we are thinking positively, we are creating a life that is desirable. The psalmist said:

Psalm 55:22
Cast thy burden upon the LORD, *and he shall sustain thee: he shall never suffer the righteous to be moved.*

We can live happy lives and sustain our health by committing each day into God's hands and asking for His grace, thereby allowing the Holy Spirit to resolve our problems and guide us in the way He would have us go. When we are truly centered in Christ, our inner conflicts can be eliminated, releasing positive energy that will improve our physical and mental health.

James Allen, author of *As A Man Thinketh*, realized this when he said: *"The power of the human mind is so strong that it makes man possess an ability to mold his personality, create his future, build his destiny, and turn*

The Role of Our Mental Attitude in Healing

his dreams into reality."[19] Likewise, if the human mind is focused on negative thoughts, including stress, anxiety, anger and resentment, this can lead to physical ailments. All of these have been shown to be a contributing factor in disorders and diseases such as cardiovascular disease, ulcers, blood pressure problems, headaches, respiratory problems[20] and even cancer.

I believe if I had heeded this advice, I would not have developed breast cancer in the first place. As I mentioned earlier, I have always felt responsible for everyone else's happiness. I felt that I could solve every problem. Then came a time in my life when I couldn't seem to keep anyone happy, and the problems of my world seemed bigger than I was. If only I had let go of my problems and let God take over!

God used breast cancer to teach me to trust in Him and to prepare me for the life He intended. Now, I can relate to what Peter wrote:

1 Peter 5:10, AMPC
And after you have suffered a little while, the God of all grace [Who imparts all blessing and favor], Who has called you to His [own] eternal glory in Christ Jesus, will Himself complete and make you what you ought to be, establish and ground you securely, and strengthen, and settle you.

---

19. Allen, James, *As a Man Thinketh* (Golgotha Press: 2011)
20. Patel, Dimpel, *How Negative Thoughts Affect Your Life*, January 11,

Thank You, God!

When we daily study the Word of God and speak to Him in prayer, it brings inner peace and insight into life's problems and decision-making. Our help is in Christ. What Paul wrote in Philippians 4:13 gives us personal security to trust the Lord for every aspect of our lives:

> *I can do all things through Christ who strengthens me.* (NKJV)

Do not become confused and frustrated with life. Let the Holy Spirit, Who lives within each of God's children, direct you through the problems of life. Jesus said:

John 14:26-27
> *But the Comforter, which is the Holy Ghost, whom the Father will send in my name, he shall teach you all things, and bring all things to your remembrance, whatsoever I have said unto you. Peace I leave with you, my peace I give unto you: not as the world giveth, give I unto you. Let not your heart be troubled, neither let it be afraid.*

We do not have to worry about the failures of yesterday. Again Jesus said:

The Role of Our Mental Attitude in Healing

Matthew 6:34, My Paraphrase
> *Don't worry about tomorrow, tomorrow will take care of itself, and don't be concerned about yesterday, you can't recall it, it is past.*

The apostle Paul instructed us:

Philippians 3:13
> *... Forgetting those things which are behind and reaching forward to those things which are ahead.*

Live for today! God will take care of your needs for tomorrow!

When God forgives, He also forgets. We must do likewise.

Luke 6:37, NKJV
> *Judge not, and you shall not be judged. Condemn not, and you shall not be condemned. Forgive, and you will be forgiven.*

1 John 1:9
> *If we confess our sins, he is faithful and just to forgive us our sins, and to cleanse us from all unrighteousness.*

Life is filled with trials and temptations, sorrows and disappointments. However, the wisdom expressed in Proverbs reminds us:

Proverbs 3:1-12, MSG

Don't lose your grip on Love and Loyalty.
  Tie them around your neck; carve their initials on your heart.
Earn a reputation for living well
in God's eyes and the eyes of the people.

Trust God from the bottom of your heart;
  don't try to figure out everything on your own.
Listen for God's voice in everything you do, everywhere you go;
  he's the one who will keep you on track.
Don't assume that you know it all.
  Run to God! Run from evil!
Your body will glow with health,
  your very bones will vibrate with life!
Honor God with everything you own;
  give him the first and the best.
Your barns will burst,
  your wine vats will brim over.
But don't, dear friend, resent God's discipline;
  don't sulk under his loving correction.
It's the child he loves that God corrects;
  a father's delight is behind all this.

Ultimately, the best way to sustain your mental and physical health is to be happy. Don't stress, don't worry. When you have been wronged, forgive and forget, and when you have done wrong, ask for forgiveness.

The Role of Our Mental Attitude in Healing

As Paul taught, we must *"pray without ceasing"* (1 Thessalonians 5:17). This means turn your cares over to the Lord. Do not worry! Remember, Jesus said:

John 10:10
I am come that ye might have life and that ye might have it more abundantly.

Remember also the wisdom of Jesus we noted in a previous chapter:

Matthew 6:25-34
Therefore I say unto you, Take no thought for your life, what ye shall eat, or what ye shall drink; nor yet for your body, what ye shall put on. Is not the life more than meat, and the body than raiment? Behold the fowls of the air: for they sow not, neither do they reap, nor gather into barns; yet your heavenly Father feedeth them. Are ye not much better than they? Which of you by taking thought can add one cubit unto his stature?

And why take ye thought for raiment? Consider the lilies of the field, how they grow; they toil not, neither do they spin: and yet I say unto you, That even Solomon in all his glory was not arrayed like one of these. Wherefore, if God so clothe the grass of the field, which today is, and tomorrow is cast into the oven, shall he not much more clothe you, O ye of little faith?

Therefore take no thought, saying, What shall we eat? or, What shall we drink? or, Wherewithal shall we be clothed? For your heavenly Father knoweth that ye have need of all these things. But seek ye first the kingdom of God, and his righteousness; and all these things shall be added unto you. Take therefore no thought for the morrow: for the morrow shall take thought for the things of itself. Sufficient unto the day is the evil thereof.

That says it all.

CHAPTER 9

The Role of Diet in Healing

"Those who fail to take the time to be healthy will ultimately have to take the time to be sick."
                              ~ **Dr. James Chappell**

The Bible tells us that God created grass, herbs and fruits on the third day of creation. He then specifically instructed us to consume them, because they were *"good"*:

Genesis 1:12
And the earth brought forth grass, and herb yielding seed after his kind, and the tree yielding fruit, whose seed was in itself, after his kind: and God saw that it was good.

Genesis 1:29
And God said, Behold, I have given you every herb bearing seed, which is upon the face of all the earth,

and every tree, in which is the fruit of a tree yielding seed; to you it shall be for meat.

The ideal diet is one rich in vegetables, fruits, grains, legumes (beans), cold-water ocean fish, olive oil and, yes, a little red wine and red meat. The healthiest diet consists of seventy percent fresh raw fruits and vegetables, nuts and seeds. Raw food is much easier for your body to digest. It passes through the digestive tract in one half to one third the time it takes for cooked food. Raw foods are also high in fiber and rich in enzymes, which are needed for the digestive system to work efficiently. Enzymes are necessary to break down food particles, so they can be utilized for energy. A lack of digestive enzymes can be a factor in food allergies, bloating, belching, gas, bowel disorders, abdominal cramping and heartburn.

Only about thirty percent of one's diet should be made up of cooked foods, grains, legumes and meats. Nearly every food preparation process reduces the amount of nutrients in food. When raw foods are exposed to temperatures above 118°, they start to rapidly break down. Many nutrients are lost in the cooking process, and once enzymes are exposed to heat, they are no longer able to provide the function for which they were designed.

Another important reason to include fruits and vegetables in one's diet is the body's need for fiber. According to the Institute of Medicine, children and adults should consume fourteen grams of fiber for

The Role of Diet in Healing

every thousand calories of food they eat each day. A fiber deficiency increases your risk of high cholesterol, cardiovascular disease, high blood sugar (which can lead to diabetes), obesity, colon cancer, hemorrhoids and constipation. Irregular bowel movements fail to properly flush waste from our body, allowing toxins to build up in our system. This toxic overload can be the cause of migraine headaches and, I have discovered, even breast cancer.

As noted previously, Physicians Nicholas L. Petrakis and Eileen B. King of the University of California, writing in the periodical *Lancet*, have found that women who have two or fewer bowel movements per week have four times the risk of breast disease (benign or malignant) as women who have one or more bowel movements per day.

When consuming nutrition-rich foods, we must ensure that the vitamins and minerals they contain will be processed completely. When too large a quantity of food is consumed at one time or when high-dosage supplements are consumed, the body cannot process the nutrition fast enough, causing precious vitamins and minerals to be lost because the body cannot absorb such large quantities at one time. Also, if there is inadequate water available to cleanse one's body tissues, a toxic buildup may result.

This danger does not exist when we introduce nutrients into the body through natural raw foods. The nutrition one consumes from food is more easily absorbed by the body.

The Word of God expressly warns against abstaining from meat because of fear or false doctrine and assures us of the goodness of all that God has created:

1 Timothy 4:1-5
> *But the Spirit saith expressly, that in later times some shall fall away from the faith, giving heed to seducing spirits and doctrines of demons, through the hypocrisy of men that speak lies, branded in their own conscience as with a hot iron; forbidding to marry, and commanding to abstain from meats, which God created to be received with thanksgiving by them that believe and know the truth. For every creature of God is good, and nothing is to be rejected, if it be received with thanksgiving: for it is sanctified through the word of God and prayer.*

Paul also instructed:

1 Corinthians 10:24-26, My Paraphrase
> *Nobody should seek his own good, but the good of others. Eat anything sold in the meat market without raising questions of conscience for "The earth is the Lord's, and everything in it."*

When traveling by ship, Paul urged his fellow travelers:

The Role of Diet in Healing

Acts 27:34

Wherefore, I pray you to take some meat: for this is for your health ... .

I know, from my own experience, that when I gave up red meat, as recommended by the Naturopath for the treatment of cancer, my energy level plummeted. I was introduced to Dr. Peter D'Adamo's book, *Eat Right 4 Your Type*,[21] and realized I was not meant to be a vegetarian. Dr. D'Adamo had interviewed 6,617 individuals who reported their results from following the Blood Type Diet for a period of just one month. That report found that three out of four people had significant improvement in a variety of health conditions. These included weight loss, improvements in digestive function, resistance to stress, overall energy and mental clarity. I have type O blood and found that I was one of those who saw a drastic improvement in my energy level and overall mood.

The survey also showed the same percentages of positive results across all blood types. Type O individuals who followed a higher protein (meat), lower carbohydrate diet were as likely to report positive results as Type A individuals, who followed a lower fat, plant-based diet, or Types B and AB individuals, who followed a more omnivorous (both plant and animal-based foods) diet.

---

21. D'Adamo, Peter J. *Eat Right 4 Your Type* (New York, NY, Berekley Books: 1996)

The apostle Mark recorded Jesus' words, again showing that everything that God created is good for food:

Mark 7:18-23, NKJV
So, He said to them, "Are you thus without understanding also? Do you not perceive that whatever enters a man from outside cannot defile him, because it does not enter his heart but his stomach, and is eliminated, thus purifying all foods." And He said, "What comes out of a man; that defiles a man. For from within, out of the heart of men, proceed evil thoughts, adulteries, fornications, murders, thefts, covetousness, wickedness, deceit, lewdness, an evil eye, blasphemy, pride, foolishness. All these evil things come from within and defile a man."

Our primary concern should be about what is in our heart and mind. What we think and speak is far more destructive to our health than the food we eat or what we drink. James Allen knew this when he quoted the Scriptures:

Proverbs 23:7
For as [a man] *thinketh in his heart, so is he.*

A sick mind, a broken heart or harbored feelings of anger or resentment will all lead in time to a diseased physical state.

The Role of Diet in Healing

First Corinthians 13 tells us that love is the most important thing, the greatest gift:

1 Corinthians 13:4-13, My Paraphrase
> *Love is patient, love is kind, it isn't jealous, it doesn't brag, it isn't arrogant, it isn't rude, it doesn't seek its own advantage, it isn't irritable, it doesn't keep a record of complaints, it isn't happy with injustice, but it is happy with the truth. Love puts up with all things, trusts in all things, hopes for all things, endures all things ... . Love never fails. Now faith, hope, and love remain—these three things—and the greatest of these is love.*

Get the spirit right, but don't forget to eat right too.

CHAPTER 10

The Role of Abstinence in Healing

1 Thessalonians 5:22
Abstain from all appearance of evil.

There are certainly instances when it is appropriate to refrain from certain foods or beverages—whether it is a vow of abstinence or during a time of fasting, cleansing or simply as part of a healing diet. Whatever the reason, our commitment needs to be taken as seriously as a vow and always and only to honor God:

Romans 14:6
... He that eateth, eateth to the Lord, for he giveth God thanks; and he that eateth not, to the Lord he eateth not, and giveth God thanks.

When someone pledges, or resolves, solemnly to strictly observe certain dietary guidelines in order to

The Role of Abstinence in Healing

give their body the necessary nutrition to heal naturally, it is crucial that they not grow weary. Rather, they must continue to pursue God's guidance and adhere to the vow they have made, believing that God will honor their commitment just as He did those in Bible days.

The Bible tells us:

Ecclesiastes 5:5, NIV
It is better not to vow than to make a vow and not fulfill it.

According to Dr. Johanna Budwig, "it is possible to restore health in a few months, at most, 90% of the time."[22] However, her research has shown "that those who break the dietary rules, eating preserved meats, candy, etc., will sometimes grow rapidly worse and cannot be saved after they come back from their spree."[23]

In the New Testament book of James, we read:

James 2:20
Faith without works is dead.

This statement confirms that faith is valueless if we fail to act on what we believe. Our heavenly Father can

---
22. https://www.cancerresearchuk.org/about-cancer/cancer-in-general/treatment/complementary-alternative-therapies/individual-therapies/budwig-diet
23. Ibid

and does perform miracles of healing. However, you and I must be willing and committed to do our part. By making healthy changes to our diet and lifestyle, we are, in essence, acting on our faith.

There are numerous accounts in the Bible of extraordinary men and women who were instructed by God to abnegate certain foods and beverages and make other physical sacrifices for a period of time, during which they would be separated unto the Lord. For example, specific instructions to those commissioned to the highest calling of Nazarite priests are listed in Numbers 6.

Those who vowed to God and adhered strictly to that vow were given great physical and spiritual strength. Judges 13-16, for instance, tells the story of the life of Samson. This man's life also illustrates the blessings are removed if a vow is no longer honored.

John the Baptist was also designated as a Nazarite priest. His amazing story is told in Luke 1. His Father, Zacharias, was told by an angel of the Lord:

Luke 1:15
> *For he shall be great in the sight of the Lord, and shall drink neither wine nor strong drink; and he shall be filled with the Holy Ghost, even from his mother's womb.*

The very first chapter of Daniel tells of a vow Daniel and his friends—Hananiah, Mishael and Azariah—made when captured by Nebuchadnezzar, King of Babylon:

The Role of Abstinence in Healing

Daniel 1:8 and 12

But Daniel purposed in his heart that he would not defile himself with the portion of the king's meat, nor with the wine which he drank … .

Let them give us pulse [raw leguminous plants, peas, beans, etc.] *to eat, and water to drink … .*

The result was that God blessed them with great wisdom and honored their vow:

Daniel 1:20

And in all matters of wisdom and understanding, that the king enquired of them, he found them ten times better than all the magicians and astrologers that were in all his realm.

The Word of God instructs us to seek the Lord's favor, not the favor of men:

Colossians 3:23-24

And whatsoever ye do, do it heartily, as to the Lord, and not unto men; knowing that of the Lord ye shall receive the reward of the inheritance: for ye serve the Lord Christ.

Often, others do not understand our vows made to honor God. Nor do they appreciate the limitations we imposes on ourself as part of a dietary commitment.

1 Corinthians 2:14
> *But the natural man receiveth not the things of the Spirit of God: for they are foolishness unto him: neither can he know them, because they are spiritually discerned.*

Examples of man's lack of understanding in this regard are shown in the way both John the Baptist and Jesus were perceived. They said John had a devil:

Luke 7:33
> *For John the Baptist came neither eating bread nor drinking wine; and ye say, He hath a devil.*

Then, when Jesus came eating and drinking, they called him a winebibber:

Luke 7:34
> *The Son of man is come eating and drinking; and ye say, Behold a gluttonous man, and a winebibber, a friend of publicans and sinners!*

Jesus freed men from Old Testament dietary restrictions, and yet He was rejected and mocked by the Pharisees and lawyers who did not believe. If we, as Christians, seek to model our lives after Christ, we, too, will be misunderstood, mocked and ridiculed. In fact, Jesus said:

The Role of Abstinence in Healing

Matthew 10:24-26, CEB

Disciples aren't greater than their teacher, and slaves aren't greater than their master. It's enough for disciples to be like their teacher and slaves like their master. If they have called the head of the house Beelzebul, it's certain that they will call the members of his household by even worse names. Therefore, don't be afraid of those people because nothing is hidden that won't be revealed, and nothing secret that won't be brought out into the open.

Psalm 104:14-15

He causeth the grass to grow for the cattle, and herb for the service of man: that he may bring forth food out of the earth; and wine that maketh glad the heart of man, and oil to make his face to shine, and bread which strengtheneth man's heart.

It is all good, but there are times when it is wiser to refrain from eating or drinking. Be led by God's Spirit.

Chapter 11

The Role of Wine and Spirits in Healing

The apostle Paul instructed Timothy:

1 Timothy 5:23
Drink no longer water, but use a little wine for thy stomach's sake and thine often infirmities.

Research has now confirmed that drinking a modest amount of wine or other alcoholic beverages is actually good for your health. It can lower your bad cholesterol, increase your good cholesterol, lower your blood pressure, increase your bone density, reduce your chance of kidney stones, increase your memory and even extend your life expectancy.

Wine, particularly those made with red grapes, contains a substance called resveratrol. This naturally-occurring phenol, which inhibits cancer growth, has a proven ability to protect against atherosclerosis and coronary heart disease. The Mayo Clinic published information stating, "The alcohol and certain substances in red wine called antioxidants may help prevent heart disease by increasing levels of 'good' cholesterol and protecting against artery damage."[24]

The medical journal *Cell Metabolism* suggested that resveratrol helps keep the bones, eyes, kidneys, heart and other muscles healthier as one ages. The recommended consumption was one or two glasses of beer or wine or one and a half ounces of liquor per day.

New Science Magazine cited a University College of London study whereby data was collected from more than twelve thousand mothers and children in the United Kingdom over a period of seven years. Apparently: "Kids whose mothers had one to two alcoholic drinks per week during pregnancy had fewer cognitive and behavioral problems by age three than those of woman who abstained."[25]

John 2 gives an account of Jesus' first miracle, that of turning water into wine. There is a second account in John 4, which says:

John 4:46

So Jesus came again into Cana of Galilee, where he made the water wine.

---

24. https://newsnetwork.mayoclinic.org/discussion/mayo-clinic-q-and-a-is-daily-drinking-problem-drinking/
25. https://snewscientist.com/

There is no negative connotation here, for Jesus did not condemn the drinking of wine. He Himself drank wine, and if He had considered it to be bad, He never would have miraculously produced more wine at the wedding ceremony when they ran out. Remember, all things that God created are *"good."*

The ceremony of Holy Communion was given to us by Christ Himself. Through it we remember and also participate in His sacrifice for us. It is observed just like the last supper He shared with His disciples, before His arrest and crucifixion. He has commanded us to observe it too:

Luke 22:19, NKJV
"Do this in remembrance of Me."

Paul later recounted the event:

1 Corinthians 11:24-26
And when he [Jesus] *had given thanks, he brake it* [the bread], *and said, Take, eat: this is my body, which is broken for you: this do in remembrance of me. After the same manner also he took the cup* [the wine], *when he had supped, saying, this cup is the new testament in my blood: this do ye, as oft as ye drink it, in remembrance of me. For as often as ye eat this bread, and drink this cup, ye do shew the Lord's death till he come.*

The Role of Wine and Spirits in Healing

Every time we partake of Holy Communion, we recall the sacrifice Jesus made for us on the cross and the promises He made:

Isaiah 53:5
> *But he was wounded for our transgressions; he was bruised for our iniquities: the chastisement of our peace was upon him; and with his stripes we are healed.*

1 Peter 2:24
> *Who his own self bare our sins in his own body on the tree, that we, being dead to sins, should live unto righteousness: by whose stripes ye were healed.*

If wine were bad for us, Jesus never would have used it in this way. Drink it moderately for your health's sake.

CHAPTER 12

The Dangers Posed by Food Additives

Jesus freed us from the dietary restrictions imposed by Old Testament Law, and the Word tells us that all fruits, vegetables, grains, seeds and meats have been made by God to be eaten and enjoyed by mankind. Unfortunately, today many of the foods and beverages we consume are laced with additives, preservatives and food coloring. The processing methods used to prepare the foods add hydrogenated oils, stabilizers and flavor enhancers that are man-made and unhealthy for human consumption. In order to increase crop production, herbicides, pesticides and chemical fertilizers are added to our soil and sprayed on the fields where our food is produced.

As a result, toxic build-up from consuming large quantities of preservatives, food additives and pesticides have been linked to developmental disorders and other serious diseases. These include but are not limited to:

The Dangers Posed by Food Additives

Cancer	Cardio-vascular disease
Impaired Immune System	Hormonal Imbalances
ADHD	Hyperactivity
Learning Disorders	Autism
Brain Fog	Obesity
Headaches	Joint Pain and Stiffness
Migraines	Anemia
Nasal Congestion and Mucus	Skin Rashes
Dark Circles under the Eyes	Brown Blotches on the Skin
Muscular Sclerosis	Rheumatoid Arthritis

Our body stores chemicals and toxins in our fatty tissue. This explains the huge increase in obesity among those who consume the greatest quantities of processed foods and the largest number of meals eaten at fast food restaurants. It has been proven that environmental toxins in fat cause obesity, diabetes and cancer.

Weight gain, however, is more than a calories problem; it is a toxin problem. According to J.K. Paulsen, M.D. a Bariatric Physician, "The body naturally manufactures fat in abundance to incarcerate and absorb chemicals and toxins that accumulate over time. As you cleanse the body, one can expect fat and inches to be substantially reduced.

"The Environmental Protection Agency has monitored human exposure to toxic environmental chemicals since 1972 when they began the National Human Adipose Tissue Survey. They found that five of what are known to be the most toxic chemicals were found in 100% of all samples. ... Nine more chemicals were found in 91-98% of samples: Polychlorinated biphenyls (PCBs) were found in 83% of the population."[26]

On the basis of this and other similar studies, I strongly recommend that everyone eat raw, organic foods and meat from wild game or grass-fed livestock when possible and avoid processed foods. Processed foods can cause serious side-effects and toxicity. On the other hand, foods consumed in their natural state give you the full benefit of God's design to keep your body in good health. The chart below has been compiled from information I discovered while doing research for my natural cancer cure. It lists some of the most common food additives and their known side effects.

After doing these studies, I became extremely careful when grocery shopping, reading labels and asking questions at the meat department and even at the farmers' market. Avoiding harmful food additives was an important step in my recover from cancer.

---

26. Mark Hyman, *Systems Biology, Toxins, Obesity, and Functional Medicine*. 13th International Symposium of The Institute for Functional Medicine

The Dangers Posed by Food Additives

WHAT IT IS	WHERE IT IS FOUND	POTENTIAL RISKS
Hormones	Meat Products, fresh and processed cow's milk and milk products (cheese, yogurt, etc)	Linked to an increased risk of breast, colon, prostate and lung cancer.[27] Has also been linked to larger than normal breasts and young girls starting periods earlier than normal.[28]
Antibiotics	Fresh and processed meat products	Linked to antibiotic resistance in humans. Has high levels of nitrofuran, an antibiotic known to cause cancer.[29]
Chlorine	Public water systems and swimming pools	Linked to the aggravation and cause of respiratory diseases like asthma. The most serious side effect is Alzheimer's disease.
Fluoride	Public water systems, toothpaste and mouth washes	Linked to cancer, diabetes, thyroid and neurological disorders, hormonal imbalances, heart disease, arthritis and osteoporosis
Aluminum	Public water systems, toothpaste and mouth washes	Linked to Parkinson-type diseases and osteoporosis and is a neuron-toxic hazard.

---

27. Jeffery M. Smith, *Genetic Roulette: The Documented Health Risks of Genetically Engineered Foods* (Fairfield, IA: Yes Books, 2007), P 157
28. Cohen, Robert, *Early Sexual Maturity and Milk Hormones,* health101.org
29. Martin Khor, *The dangers of antibiotics in animal feed,* Third World Network

Glutamino acid (MSG) Monosodium Glutamate	Found in many processed foods, it is often listed as a spice in the ingredient list.	Linked to behavioral problems in children, attention deficit hyperactivity disorder (ADHD) or emotional problems. Children often undergo a remarkable change when MSG is eliminated from their diet.
Benzene (preservative)	Often found in beverages that contain both ascorbic acid (vitamin C) and sodium benzoate	A known carcinogen, Benzene causes harmful effects on the bone marrow and can cause a decrease in red blood cells, leading to anemia. Can also cause excessive bleeding and can affect the immune system.[30]
Artificial sweeteners	Packaged and processed foods, diet foods and sugar-free foods	Linked to cancers, hyperactivity/ADHD/learning disabilities
Methylene chloride, a solvent used to remove caffeine from coffee	Decaffeinated coffee	A proven carcinogenic that is toxic to lungs, the nervous system, liver, mucous membranes and the central nervous system (CNS). Repeated or prolonged exposure to the substance can produce organ damage.[31]

---

30. Avianweb.com/diseasescausedbytoxin.html
31. Ibid

The Dangers Posed by Food Additives

Tartrazine aka FD&C Yellow No:5; CI Acid Yellow 23, CI Food Yellow 4. Coal tar dye	Sodas, sweets, jams, cereals, snack foods, canned fish and packaged soups	Cancer probability. Known to provoke asthma attacks and urticaria (nettle rash) in children. May cause altered states of perception and behavior, uncontrolled hyper-agitation and confusion and wakefulness in young children. Also known to inhibit zinc metabolism and interfere with digestive enzymes
Yellow 2G, Acid yellow 17, CI Food yellow 5, Coal tar dye, artificial color	Soft drinks	May cause asthma, rashes and hyperactivity
Sunset yellow FCF, Orange yellow S, FD&C yellow No:6, CI food yellow 3 (artificial color)	Cereals, bakery sweets, snack foods, ice cream, candy, drinks, canned fish, orange squash, jelly, jam, cakes, soups, desert mixes, yoghurt and sauces	Can provoke allergic reactions, such as abdominal pain, hyperactivity, hives and nasal congestion. Potentially dangerous to asthmatics. Causes bronchial constriction, kidney tumors and chromosomal damage. It also produces urticaria, swelling of the blood vessels and gastric upset.
FD&C Red No:40 artificial orange-red color	Sweets, cakes, biscuits, drinks, condiments and even medications	Has been connected with cancer and organ damage
Indigotine, Indigo carmine, FD&C Blue No2, synthetic coal tar dye, artificial color	Milk deserts, sweets, biscuits, ice creams, baked goods and confectionery	May cause nausea, vomiting, high blood pressure, skin rashes, breathing problems, brain tumors and other allergic reactions[32]

---

32. Ibid

| Brilliant blue FCF, FD&C blue dye No:1, CI acid blue 9, CI food blue 2, CI pigment blue 24, artificial color | Dairy products, sweets and drinks | Can cause hyperactivity, skin rashes, chromosomal damage and bronchial constriction |

You owe it to yourself and your family to become a wise shopper and consumer. We only have one life to live. Protect it.

Chapter 13

The Role of Water in Healing

The Bible speaks of water hundreds of times. The Word of God is referred to as the *Living Water*. Jesus said:

John 7:38, NKJV
He who believes in Me, as the Scripture has said, out of his heart will flow rivers of living water.

It is through the baptism with water that grace is conferred on a believer. No matter what is in a person's past, baptism starts anew the covenantal relationship between God and the person being baptized.
John the Baptist said:

Matthew 3:11
I indeed baptize you with water unto repentance, but He who is coming after me is mightier than I, whose

sandals I am not worthy to carry. He will baptize you with the Holy Spirit and fire.

Water was also used repeatedly in miraculous healings in the Bible:

John 9:11
He answered and said, A man that is called Jesus made clay, and anointed mine eyes, and said unto me, Go to the pool of Siloam, and wash: and I went and washed, and I received sight.

John 5:2-4
Now there is at Jerusalem by the sheep market a pool, which is called in the Hebrew tongue Bethesda .... In these lay a great multitude of impotent folk, of blind, halt, withered, waiting for the moving of the water. For an angel went down at a certain season into the pool, and troubled the water: whosoever then first after the troubling of the water stepped in was made whole of whatsoever disease he had.

Water has long been known to promote health due to its restorative and detoxifying properties. In fact, without water, life is impossible. Every living thing depends on water to survive. The human body is estimated to be about sixty to seventy percent water. Blood is eighty-three percent water. Our brain is seventy-seven to seventy-eight percent water. We human beings can

The Role of Water in Healing

only survive without water for approximately three days, as our body needs to constantly replace the water lost due to perspiration and normal bodily functions.

In order to remain healthy, one's daily diet needs to include a minimum of one ounce of water for every two pounds of body weight. (For example, approximately eight eight-ounce glasses of water are required for an individual weighing 128 pounds.) Without adequate water intake, the body cannot regulate its temperature or provide the means for nutrients to travel to all of its organs. Water also transports oxygen to our cells, removes waste and protects our joints and organs.

Fortunately, the foods we consume contribute to our water intake. Leafy vegetables, root vegetables and sprouts generally consist of ninety to ninety-five percent water, and fruits contain eighty to ninety percent water. Therefore, by eating one cup of vegetables or fruit, you will consume almost a cup of water.[33]

Dairy products are also a great source of water. Milk itself is eighty-eight percent water, yogurt is eighty percent water. By consuming eight to sixteen ounces of milk products per day, one is able to easily increase their fluid intake. Replacing cow's milk with fresh goat's milk can give you a complete protein source which contains all the essential amino acids as well as calcium and vitamin C.

---

33. Brooke, Dorothea, *Meeting Hydration without actually drinking water*, Associated content, Institute of Medicine of the National Academies, August 28, 2007

Goat's milk is one of the best-known foods for regenerating the cells of the body. It is also well known as a healing remedy for stomach, colon, intestinal and arthritic-like conditions. It is one of the best foods for rebuilding the nervous system and brain and improving mental function. Another added benefit of goat's milk is that it is much lower in fat content than cow's milk. Its fat globules are one ninth the size of cow's milk, which makes goat's milk easier to digest, and it is naturally homogenized.

Dry ingredients such as beans, grains, rice and pasta also become water-rich foods when they are cooked. This is because they act as sponges, absorbing the the water in which they are prepared. A cup of these products also contains nearly two-thirds of a cup of water. Even lean meats, especially poultry and fish, are generally sixty-two to seventy percent water.

Caffeine and caffeinated beverages such as coffee, tea, soft drinks and energy drinks, act as diuretics, which hastens the excretion of water from one's body. Therefore, caffeinated beverages cannot be included when considering your water intake because you will actually lose (through urination) more water than you consume due to the diuretic effect of the caffeine.

A common side-effect of the over-consumption of diuretics or caffeinated beverages is the loss of potassium and magnesium. Listed below are some of the serious side-effects of low potassium levels, including but not limited to:

The Role of Water in Healing

- fatigue
- muscle weakness and cramps
- intestinal paralysis, which may lead to bloating
- constipation

The best foods to replenish your body's potassium levels include:

- cold-water ocean fish
- carrots
- oranges
- prunes
- tomatoes
- apricots
- avocados
- bananas
- dates
- figs

Low magnesium levels can cause some or all of the following:

- sensitivity to noise
- nervousness
- irritability
- mental depression
- confusion
- twitching
- trembling

- apprehension
- insomnia
- muscle weakness and cramps in the toes, feet, legs or fingers

The best foods to restore your body's magnesium levels include:

- whole-grain breads and cereals
- beans
- corn
- nuts
- bananas
- cocoa
- dark green vegetables

It has been documented that many serious health conditions are linked to dehydration. Some of the most common are listed below. If you suffer from any of the following conditions, you may very well be dehydrated and, therefore, could cure your condition by simply drinking enough water and increasing your intake of high moisture, nutritious foods.

Conditions Linked to Dehydration

- dermatitis
- constipation
- diabetes

The Role of Water in Healing

- dry skin and hair
- high blood pressure
- indigestion
- obesity
- osteoporosis
- tension headaches
- muscle cramps
- restless leg syndrome
- fatigue

There is growing scientific evidence linking increased water intake with a reduced risk of major illnesses. Consuming adequate amounts of water significantly reduces the risk of developing kidney stones and is also instrumental in the prevention of cancer and heart disease.

The easiest way to monitor whether or not you are getting enough water is to keep an eye on the color of your urine. Very pale yellow urine ensures that you are well hydrated. If your urine color strays into darker tones, particularly if it starts to smell a bit, it's time to reach for a glass of water.

> **FOR BODILY EXERCISE PROFITS A LITTLE, BUT GODLINESS IS PROFITABLE FOR ALL THINGS, HAVING PROMISE OF THE LIFE THAT NOW IS AND OF THAT WHICH IS TO COME.**
> 1 Timothy 4:8

Chapter 14

The Role of Exercise in Healing

Jeremiah 9:24
> ... Exercise loving kindness, judgment, and righteousness, in the earth: for in these things I delight, saith the LORD.

This, of course, speaks of a spiritual exercise. The Bible does specifically speak of physical exercise:

1 Timothy 4:7-8
> But refuse profane and old wives' fables, and exercise thyself rather unto godliness. For bodily exercise is profitable for a little; but godliness is profitable for all things, having promise of the life which now is, and of that which is to come.

The Word of God instructs that our faith and trust should be in the Lord, not in the food we eat or in some strict regimen of exercise, and yet throughout the Bible, the words *"work"* and *"walk"* are used hundreds of times. God intends for us to be active in our faith and in our daily physical lives.

James 2:20
Faith without works is dead.

Isaiah 57:2, NKJV
He shall enter into peace;
They shall rest in their beds,
Each one walking in his uprightness.

Research has shown that people who live active lives, especially those who walk regularly, have fewer incidences of cancer, heart disease, stroke, diabetes and many other debilitating diseases. Active people live longer, and they enjoy continued mental health and experience great spiritual benefits.

The benefits of exercise are obvious, especially important in this day and age with so many sedentary jobs offering limited activity. Much of today's leisure time is also sedentary, dominated by the use of computers, telephones and televisions. A lack of physical activity has contributed to a generation of obesity and disease.

Listed below is a sampling of some of the health conditions that will be improved, many even cured, by a simple exercise regimen:

The Role of Exercise in Healing

- Improves digestion
- Enhances the quality of sleep (A good night's sleep can improve your concentration, productivity and mood.)
- Helps bring calmness (A brisk thirty-minute walk helps us calm down after some stressful event.)
- Increases muscle strength and energy
- Enables weight loss and keeps wight off by burning extra calories.
- Helps prevent Type 2 diabetes by improving your body's ability to use insulin. (Normally, insulin is released from the pancreas when the amount of sugar [glucose] in the blood increases, such as after eating. Insulin stimulates the liver and muscles to take in excess glucose. This results in a lowering of the blood sugar level. When exercising, the body needs extra energy or fuel (in the form of glucose) for the activated muscles. With continued moderate exercise, your muscles take up glucose at almost twenty times the normal rate. This lowers blood sugar levels.)
- Improves mental focus and concentration
- Reduces your risk for diseases such as Alzheimer's and senility (Regular exercise, especially weight-bearing exercise, reduces the risk of osteoporosis, and can even reverse it by building bone tissue!)
- Reduces the risk of breast cancer by up to sixty percent. (Estradiol and progesterone, two ovarian

hormones which are linked to breast cancer tumor production, are lowered in the body by exercise. Fat has long been known to be a catalyst in the production of estrogen [estradiol]. Regular exercise burns body fat, thus decreasing the rate of estrogen production and the risk of breast cancer.)

- Makes you more limber and improves endurance
- Increases your endorphins, your "feel good" hormones. (Nothing improves mood and suppresses depression better than endorphins.)
- Improves circulation and helps reduce blood pressure
- Alleviates menstrual cramps
- Enhances coordination and balance
- Improves posture
- Helps manage high blood pressure and improves cholesterol levels
- Boosts high-density lipoprotein (HDL, the "good" cholesterol) while decreasing triglycerides
- Eases and even eliminates some back problems and pain
- Keeps your blood flowing smoothly by lowering the buildup of plaque in your arteries
- Reduces joint discomfort and makes the body more agile
- Increases your range of motion
- Enhances the immune system, thereby reducing your risk of infection and the likelihood of contracting a cold or flu

The Role of Exercise in Healing

- Improves liver function, which aids in detoxification (Physical activity delivers oxygen and nutrients to your tissues. In fact, regular physical activity helps your entire cardiovascular system. The circulation of blood through your heart and blood vessels makes them work more efficiently. And when your heart and lungs work more efficiently, you'll have more energy.)
- Helps to alleviate varicose veins

Everyone would benefit from finding a physical activity they enjoy and engaging in it for at least twenty minutes three times a week. Don't make the mistake some do, overdoing the exercise and actually harming their joints and muscles. As with everything else, use wisdom.

Chapter 15

The Role of Sunlight in Healing

The first chapter of Genesis records the days of creation. On the fourth day, it says:

Genesis 1:16-18
God made two great lights; the greater light to rule the day, and the lesser light to rule the night: he made the stars also. And God set them in the firmament of the heaven to give light upon the earth, and to rule over the day and over the night, and to divide the light from the darkness: and God saw that it was good.

God made the sun, and everything He made is *"good"* and to be enjoyed by His people.

Ecclesiastes 5:18
Behold that which I have seen: it is good and comely for one to eat and to drink, and to enjoy the good of

The Role of Sunlight in Healing

all his labour that he taketh under the sun all the days of his life, which God giveth him: for it is his portion.

The human body was designed by God to synthesize vitamin D in the skin when exposed to ultraviolet B (UVB) radiation from the sun. Sunlight exposure provides us with our entire vitamin D requirement. Unfortunately, there is a growing impact on the production of vitamin D in the body because of the widespread use of sunscreen. According to the Linus Pauling Institute, "The application of sunscreen with an SPF factor of 8 reduces production of vitamin D by 95%."[34]

Vitamin D helps maintain bone density and healthy bone growth and helps maintain the normal functioning of the nervous system. It is crucially important in aiding the body's absorption of calcium. Without sufficient vitamin D, calcium supplements are almost useless. Vitamin D insufficiency is a contributing factor in osteoporosis, as calcium absorption cannot be maximized. Vitamin D's purpose is to maintain calcium levels in the blood in the normal range and to tell the body to absorb more calcium from food as needed. Osteoporosis is strongly associated with low Vitamin D levels.

Doctors know that low levels of vitamin D are linked to certain kinds of cancers, as well as to diabetes and asthma. Now, new research also shows that vitamin D can kill human cancer cells.

---
34. https://lpi.oregonstate.edu/mic/vitamins/vitamin-D

JoEllen Welsh, a researcher with the State University of New York at Albany, has studied the effects of vitamin D for twenty-five years now. She found that when human breast cancer cells were treated with vitamin D, within a few days, half of the cancer cells had shriveled up and died. "What happens is that vitamin D enters the cells and triggers the cell death process," she told *Good Morning America*. "It's similar to what we see when we treat cells with Tamoxifen [a drug used to treat breast cancer],[35] but without the side effects."

In Traditional Chinese Medicine (TCM), cancer is often viewed as a symptom of a circulation problem. This hypothesis is strengthened by the fact that many factors that decrease the risk of cancer also thin the blood. These include sunshine, exercise, aspirin use, heparin (a prescription anticoagulant), antibiotics, olive oil, fish oil, turmeric, vitamin E and garlic.[36]

Research also shows that Vitamin D is extremely important in regulating the immune system and controlling the expression of thousands of genes. Vitamin D deficiency could be a major contributing factor to the current epidemic of cancer and diabetes. It has also been found that a higher intake of vitamin D can help lower the risk of certain cancers such as breast, prostate and colorectal. The lack of Vitamin D

---
35. Clarke, Suzan, ABC News, *In Tests, Vitamin D Shrinks Breast Cancer Cells*, February 22, 2010
36. http://www.ctds.info/natthinners.html

The Role of Sunlight in Healing

contributes to chronic fatigue and depression and to Seasonal Affective Disorder (SAD). It also is the cause of some cases of congenital heart failure. The article, *"Mothers to be, better get your Vitamin D,"*[37] outlines the case that prenatal vitamin D deficiency may be linked to problems later in life such as:

- Schizophrenia
- Osteoporosis
- Decayed teeth

The chart below lists some of the best food sources of Vitamin D:

Goat's Milk	Fortified Milk Products
Cod Liver Oil	Butter
Lard	Lamb Liver
Atlantic Herring	Beef Tallow
Eastern Oysters	Pork and Beef Liver
Catfish	Beef Tripe
Skinless Sardines	Beef Kidney
Canned Mackerel	Chicken Livers
Smoked Chinook Salmon	Small Clams
Sturgeon	Blue Crab
Shrimp	Crayfish/Crawdads
Egg Yolk (One yolk contains about 24 IU)	Northern Lobster

Sun exposure of at least ten to fifteen minutes three times a week during the spring, summer and fall, in the middle of the day, from 11 a.m. to 2 p.m., on the

---

37. https://www.selfgrowth.com/articles/mothers_to_be_better_get_your_vitamin_d

face and arms, will provide enough vitamin D for the average individual. This sun exposure will also allow for storage of excess vitamin D during the winter when UVB rays will not reach some areas.

For people who live in latitudes around 40° north or 40° south of the equator, there is insufficient UVB radiation available for the skin to synthesize enough into vitamin D during the winter months. Vitamin D is fat soluble, which means it can be stored in your body for times when sun exposure is not available.

It is possible, when taking supplements, to overdose on Vitamin D, which causes toxicity. However, an overdose on Vitamin D never occurs with naturally occurring vitamin D in foods or from sunlight.

Ecclesiastes 11:7
Truly the light is sweet, and a pleasant thing it is for the eyes to behold the sun.

Make yourself available to the sun, and God will do the rest.

REST IN THE LORD, AND WAIT PATIENTLY FOR HIM.
Psalm 37:7

CHAPTER 16

The Role of Rest in Healing

Sleep is essential to good health because it refreshes the body and the mind. If you get enough sleep regularly every night, you will feel restored, refreshed and able to work better. During our waking hours, our nerve cells are constantly active and become fatigued. Sleep gives the cells of our body an opportunity to repair themselves.

The first book of the Bible, Genesis, tells us that even God rested after creating the earth:

Genesis 2:1-2
> *Thus the heavens and the earth were finished, and all the host of them. And on the seventh day God ended his work which he had made; and he rested on the seventh day from all his work which he had made. And God blessed the seventh day, and sanctified it: because that in it he had rested from all his work which God created and made.*

The Role of Rest in Healing

After this, God instructed His children to rest on the Sabbath and to allow their servants, the strangers living in the land, and even their cattle to rest:

Exodus 35:2, NIV
> *For six days, work is to be done, but the seventh day shall be your holy day, a day of sabbath rest to the* Lord,

Leviticus 23:3, NIV
> *There are six days when you may work, but the seventh day is a day of sabbath rest, a day of sacred assembly. You are not to do any work; wherever you live, it is a sabbath to the* Lord.

Deuteronomy 5:14, NIV
> *But the seventh day is a Sabbath to the Lord your God. On it you shall not do any work, neither you, nor your son or daughter, nor your manservant or maidservant, nor your ox, your donkey or any of your animals, nor the alien within your gates, so that your manservant and maidservant may rest, as you do.*

Exodus 34:21, NIV
> *Six days you shall labor, but on the seventh day you shall rest; even during the plowing season and harvest you must rest.*

Without adequate rest, a person may experience a significant reduction in performance and alertness by as much as thirty-two percent. Your cognitive ability—how you think and process information—is also reduced. Inadequate rest is also associated with numerous serious medical illnesses, including but not limited to the following:

- High blood pressure
- Cardiovascular disease
- Stroke
- Obesity
- Diabetes
- Psychiatric problems, including depression and other mood disorders, even Attention Deficit Disorder (ADD)
- Mental impairment
- Fetal and childhood growth retardation[38]

We were created with the ability to heal and recover from disease while we rest. It is during deep sleep that the production of growth hormone is at its peak. Growth hormone speeds the absorption of nutrients and amino acids into our cells and aids the healing of tissues throughout our body.

This hormone also stimulates our bone marrow, where our immune system cells are born. Researchers

---

38. Breus, Michael J., PhD, MD, Chronic Sleep Deprivation May Harm Health, WebMD

The Role of Rest in Healing

at the National Cancer Institute have reported that women who consistently sleep less than seven hours a night have a forty-seven percent higher risk of developing cancer.

Melatonin, often called the sleep hormone, is also produced during sleep. This hormone inhibits tumors from growing, prevents viral infections, stimulates one's immune system, increases antibodies in our saliva, has antioxidant properties and enhances the quality of sleep.[39]

According to the National Sleep Foundation, the average adult requires seven to nine hours of sleep each night. Children require even more. The most effective hours to sleep are between 10 p.m. and 6 a.m. In order to receive the full benefit of proper rest, your room should be well-ventilated, completely dark and quiet.

Adequate rest is so important to our overall health that it has been ordered by God. The Bible assures us repeatedly that God is with us *as* we rest. In fact, peaceful rest is a gift *from* Him:

Proverbs 3:24-26, NIV
When you lie down, you will not be afraid;
　when you lie down, your sleep will be sweet.
Have no fear of sudden disaster
　or of the ruin that overtakes the wicked,
for the L ORD *will be your confidence*
　　and will keep your foot from being snared.

---
39. William Collinge, M.P.H., Ph.D., *Sleep's Healing Properties*, August 25, 1999

Don't fall into the modern-day trap of occupying yourself so much that you don't have time to rest properly. God has ordered you to rest, so don't risk disobeying Him in this regard. To do so, is to risk your health.

Chapter 17

The Role of Meditation in Healing

Jesus frequently sought a solitary place to spend time alone with His Father.

Mark 1:35, NIV
Very early in the morning while it was still dark, Jesus got up, left the house, and went off to a solitary place where he prayed.

Spending time with God, in silence and solitude, meditating on His Word, helps a person become physically healthier. It creates a sense of peace, joy and contentment, while allowing us to develop a stronger relationship with our Lord and Savior. Meditation has even been medically proven to reduce stress and promote calm and a sense of inner peace. It can eliminate or reduce the symptoms of many health issues.

Christian meditation is a form of prayer in which a structured attempt is made to get in touch with and deliberately reflect on the revelations of God. The word *meditation* comes from the Latin word *meditari*, which means "to concentrate, to muse, or rehearse in one's mind." Christian meditation is also the process of deliberately focusing on specific thoughts. Specifically we are to meditate on the Word of God day and night:

Joshua 1:8
This book of the law shall not depart out of thy mouth; but thou shalt meditate therein day and night, that thou mayest observe to do according to all that is written therein: for then thou shalt make thy way prosperous, and then thou shalt have good success.

Meditation refocuses us away from ourselves and the world around us and onto God's Word, His nature, His abilities and His works. Christians are to reflect on God's Word, which is *"God-breathed"*:

2 Timothy 3:16-17, NIV
All Scripture is God-breathed and is useful for teaching, rebuking, correcting and training in righteousness, so that the servant of God may be thoroughly equipped for every good work.

The Role of Meditation in Healing

Christian meditation has nothing to do with practices that have Eastern mysticism as their foundation. Unlike Eastern meditation practices (the purpose of which is to empty oneself of daily concerns), the Christian is seeking a closer experience, or relationship, with God:

Psalm 46:10
Be still, and know that I am God.

The only true path to peace and fulfillment is through God.

Isaiah 26:3, My Paraphrase
You will keep in perfect peace him whose mind is steadfast, because he trusts in you.

James 4:8, NKJV
Draw near to God and He will draw near to you.

Take time to be alone and be quiet, and then listen, and God can speak to your mind. When He puts an idea into our mind, we call it *inspiration*. During meditation, we ask God to give us understanding through the Holy Spirit, Who has promised to lead us:

John 16:13, NKJV
When He, the Spirit of truth, has come, He will guide you into all truth.

Romans 12:2
And be not conformed to this world: but be ye transformed by the renewing of your mind, that ye may prove what is that good, and acceptable, and perfect, will of God.

Ephesians 4:23
And be renewed in the spirit of your mind.

When these basic requirements for health are provided and we keep our focus on God's will for our life, the self-healing mechanisms of our body work to restore and/or optimize our health. Our body's ability to heal itself and restore energy and vitality are a gift from God.

The apostle John stated God's will in this matter:

3 John 1:2
Beloved, I wish above all things that thou mayest prosper and be in health, even as thy soul prospereth.

Make time in your busy day to meditate on things that are eternal, thus connecting with the Eternal One.

Chapter 18

Understanding Our Body's pH Level

The term *pH* is the abbreviation for "potential Hydrogen." The higher the pH reading, the more alkaline and oxygen-rich our blood is. The lower the pH reading, the more acidic and oxygen-deprived it is. If a person has cancer, their pH reading will be very acidic or a bright yellow on a pH test strip.

Our blood should stay in a very narrow pH range (right around 7.35—7.45). Below or above this range indicates disease. The Bible emphasizes just how important our blood is. Again quoting from Leviticus:

Leviticus 17:11
For the life of the flesh is in the blood.

You can test your pH simply by wetting a piece of litmus paper with your saliva. You can purchase pH strips or litmus paper online or at most health food stores. The best time to check the pH in your saliva is two hours after a meal or upon arising before anything has been put into your mouth. A reading lower than 6.4 is indicative of insufficient alkaline reserves. If this occurs, the body has alkaline mineral deficiencies (mainly calcium and magnesium) and will not assimilate food very well. To deviate from ideal salivary pH for an extended time invites illness.[40]

The term *acidosis* is when your body remains in an acid pH state for an extended period of time. This can result in rheumatoid arthritis, lupus, tuberculosis, high blood pressure, cancers of all types, anxiety, diarrhea, dilated pupils, early-morning fatigue, headaches, hyper-activity, hyper-sexuality, nervousness, rapid heartbeat, restless leg syndrome, shortness of breath, strong cravings for sweets, dry hands and feet, diabetes, osteoporosis and insomnia.

In order to balance your pH, your diet should focus on fresh raw fruits and vegetables, and you should drink mineral water. Eliminate strong acidifiers from your diet, such as sodas, wheat and white sugar. And limit red meat consumption. One of the best ways to raise one's body pH is by making sure that adequate minerals, particularly calcium, are present in your diet. In general, green vegetables are high in calcium. Kale, broccoli and collard greens are good sources of calcium.

You can also use a urinary pH Test. This test indicates how the body is working to maintain the proper

---
40. http://www.falconblanco.com/health/alimentation/ph.htm

Understanding Our Body's pH Level

pH level of the blood. Do not test your urinary pH first thing in the morning because your body is less hydrated after a night's rest. This will cause the reading to be more acidic. It is best to test your urinary pH at least two hours after a meal. The pH of urine indicates the efforts of the body via the kidneys, adrenals, lungs and gonads to regulate pH through the buffer salts and hormones.

The ideal pH range is 5.8 to 6.8.[41] If your urinary pH stays too low, your diet should focus on foods considered to be alkaline-forming and, thus, helpful to people with consistently acid pH. These include things like almonds (raw), aloe vera, apples, apricots, beans, bee pollen, buckwheat, cabbage, cantaloupe, celery, carrots, cucumbers, dairy products like hard cheese, goat's milk, dates, dulse, eggs (poached), figs, grapefruit, honey, lemons, lettuce, millet, mineral water, miso soup, parsley, raisins, brown rice, peaches, red potatoes, pineapple, sprouted seeds, spinach (cooked) and turnip tops.

Alkaline Forming Foods

A balanced pH is critical for human health. Consuming an excessive amount of highly acidic foods and beverages, emotional stress and toxic overload caused by an impaired immune system will cause your body's pH to become acidic. And, as noted, an

---
41. http://www.alkalizeforhealth.net/salivaphtest.htm

imbalance in the pH of your body is the precursor to illness and disease.

One method the body uses to restore a proper pH balance is to pull alkaline minerals out of our bones, which are great storehouses of calcium and other alkaline minerals, and use those minerals to neutralize the acidic foods and beverages that have been consumed. The consumption of soft drinks is well-known to cause the depletion of minerals from the body's bones. This results in loss of bone mass density and the onset of osteoporosis. The more soft drinks a person consumes the weaker their bones become.

High-protein/low-carbohydrate diets are also highly acidic because red meats are very acidic. That is why a percentage of the weight loss on a nutritionally poor, low-carbohydrate diet actually results from loss of bone mass not loss of body fat!

Another way the body attempts to neutralize excess dietary acids is by increasing respiration because carbon dioxide is acidic and oxygen is alkaline. By breathing in more oxygen and exhaling more carbon dioxide, the body works to regulate its own pH.

When our pH level remains acidic for an extended period of time, it will:

- Decrease the body's ability to absorb minerals and other nutrients
- Decrease the cell's energy production
- Decrease the cell's ability to repair damage

Understanding Our Body's pH Level

- Decrease the body's ability to detoxify heavy metals, which make tumor cells thrive (This makes a person more susceptible to fatigue and illness).

The main cause of acidosis is diet. If it is too high in acid-producing animal products (like meat, eggs and dairy products), processed foods (like white flour and refined white sugar) and acid-producing beverages, (like coffee and soft drinks), your system will become unbalanced. In order to restore your body to a healthy balance, more alkaline-producing foods, like fresh fruits and vegetables and whole grains and legumes, need to be added to your daily diet.

Another culprit that causes excess acidity is the consumption of large quantities of acid-producing prescriptions and over-the-counter drugs. These are very acid forming.

A third cause of acidity is the excessive use of artificial chemical sweeteners like NutraSweet®, Spoonful®, Sweet 'N Low®, Equal® or Aspartame®. All of these are extremely acid-forming. Evidence suggests that aspartame is linked to specific health problems, including headaches, gas, confusion and brain tumors.[42]

If you have a health problem, most likely you are acidic. Research shows that unless the body's pH level is slightly alkaline, the body cannot heal itself. So, no

---
42. Roberts, 1990; Olney and others, 1996

matter what type of treatment you choose to use to take care of your health problem, it won't be effective until your pH level is back in balance. If your body's pH is not balanced, you cannot effectively assimilate vitamins, minerals and food supplements. Your body's pH level affects everything.

Research has proven that diseases [even cancer] cannot survive in an alkaline environment. On the other hand, disease and cancer cells thrive in an acidic, oxygen-deprived environment.

There are two factors that are always present with cancer, no matter what else may be present. These two factors are: acidic pH and lack of oxygen. Cancer cells cannot survive in an oxygen-rich environment. Cancer and all other diseases hate oxygen and balanced pH levels. The proper alkalinity pH of the blood (7.35—7.45) is critical for the overall health of the body.

Balancing the pH is a major step toward wellbeing and greater health. Acidosis (an overly acidic body) is the primary indicator of Calcium Deficiency Disease. Scientists have discovered that the bodily fluids of healthy people are alkaline (a high pH level), whereas the bodily fluids of sick people are acidic (a low pH level). An acidic body, therefore, is a sickness magnet.

To maintain health, your diet should consist of sixty percent alkaline-forming foods and forty percent acid-forming foods. To restore health, the diet should

Understanding Our Body's pH Level

consist of eighty percent alkaline-forming foods and twenty percent acid-forming foods.

If you are drinking diet soda, which contains aspartame, or using sugar-free products such as diet sodas or foods labeled "sugarless," "sugar free," "diet food," "low calorie," and the like, you need to read the label to see if they contain aspartame. Check labels carefully. Aspartame is extremely acid-forming and should be avoided.

Be kind to your body. It's the only one you have.

CHAPTER 19

The Necessary Dental Focus

Some years ago, during my study of oriental medicine, I became aware of acupuncture meridians and how our teeth and body are interconnected. Our teeth can have a direct influence on the organs of our body. Each tooth is related to an acupuncture meridian, which, in turn, is related to various organs, tissues and glands throughout our body. These meridians are referred to in oriental medicine as the "energy highway." The connection is so obvious that your overall health and wellness can be assessed by reviewing the condition of your teeth.

I have never been able to have children and always wondered why. Because I love kids, I thought I would have a dozen! What I found out about teeth and their relationship with other organ systems encouraged my continued research. I discovered that tooth #8, the first incisor, has direct association to conceptual

The Necessary Dental Focus

connections, hormonal capacity, impotence, sterility and other health conditions.[43] Wow! What a revelation that was!

On Christmas day in 1970, my younger brother, Tommy, received a mini-bike. He just loved that bike, and it looked like so much fun that I couldn't wait to try it out for myself. He gave me opportunity to drive it, and it was indeed great fun ... until I tried to stop. I flew right over the handlebars and into the gravel, face first, knocking out my front tooth. Little did I know that this event, that occurred when I was fourteen, probably sealed my fate and prevented me from ever having children!

I also learned that root canals are harmful to one's overall health. Unfortunately, I already had two root canals, and, because of the expense involved in having them removed, I never made extracting them a priority. That was a bad decision! The two teeth involved were tooth #3, the first molar (directly associated with the mammary gland on the left side of the body), and tooth #4, the second premolar (related to the motility and peristalsis in the small and large intestine).

That was another revelation! My history of chronic constipation could very well have been caused by the root canal I had done in 1972 when I was only sixteen. Then, sometime between 1995 and 1998, I had the second root canal done. That very well may have

---

[43]. American Bio-Compatible Health Systems, Inc. 2009, http:// naturaldentistry.us/holistic-dentistry/meridian-tooth-chart-from-encinitasdentist/

been what started the chain of events that finally led to breast cancer.

The evidence seems overwhelming. In my life, I have experienced three different dental problems and three different health conditions. The fact that the acupuncture meridians are linked from each of my problem teeth to the organ system that afflicted my body proves to me that they are, in fact, interconnected. No one can convince me that this was just a coincidence.

When I was diagnosed with cancer, my only solution was to have my root canals, my cap and all the dental amalgam removed from my teeth and replaced with all-natural materials. There is a specialized type of dentist, a "biological" or "holistic" dentist, and that is the only type of dentist who should be contacted for proper removal of root canals and the replacement of caps and fillings. A biological dentist will use precautionary methods to prevent toxins from being released into the body and will use only natural and safe material.

If it had not been for the willingness of our friends to loan us the money for my treatment, I would not have been able to afford to have this vitally important but expensive dental work performed.

According to the Independent Cancer Research Foundation, root canals are a haven for microbes. No blood can reach the inside of the root canal, which prevents one's immune system from killing any microbes inside the dead tooth.[44]

---
44. http://www.new-cancer-treatments.org/Articles/RootCanals.html

The Necessary Dental Focus

Dr. Thomas Rau, who ran the Paracelsus Cancer Clinic in Switzerland since 1958, checked the records of 150 breast cancer patients treated in his clinic. He found that 147 of them (98%) had one or more root canals on the same meridian as the original breast cancer tumor.

There are approximately twenty-four million root canals done in the U.S. every year. In a 1925 study conducted by Dr. Weston Price and sixty other prominent researchers, these dental procedures were proven to be deadly disease agents. That study has been suppressed since that time by the American Dental Association [ADA] and the American Association of Endodontists (AAE).

George Meinig, DDS, FACD, an endodontist, helped found the AAE in 1943. After practicing his craft for fifty years, he retired in 1993. He discovered the Weston Price research shortly after his retirement and concluded there is no safe way to do a root canal. He subsequently wrote the book, *Root Canal Cover-Up*,[45] first published in 1993, as a *'mea culpa'* to the thousands of patients whose health he ruined by doing root canals on them. (I suggest that you read Dr. George Meinig's book for the full story.) He has also lectured widely since then (1993), trying to alert people to this extreme danger to their health.[46]

---

45. (Santa Barbara, CA, Price-Pottenger Nutrition Foundation: 2008)
46. http://v.mercola.com/blogs/public_blog/Cancer-Continues-to-Worsen-8023.aspx

John Diamond, a medical doctor, has said, "I have had a number of patients with breast cancer, all of whom had root canals on the tooth related to the breast area on the associated energy meridian."[47] It is impossible to cure diseases unless all of the root canal teeth are removed properly by a naturopathic or biological dentist. Even if you killed the microbes of the disease, the microbes hiding in the root canals can come out and re-infect the person!

Cancer, some cases of Type 1 diabetes and a whole host of other diseases are caused by microbes, viruses, bacteria and fungi, such as yeasts and molds. To cure these diseases, the microbes must first be killed throughout the body so that the immune system can restore the body to its normal state.[48]

If that was an eye-opener for you, as it was for me, take heed and do what is necessary to protect your health.

---

47. John Diamond, M.D., Triad Medical Centre, 4600 Kietzke Lane, M-242, Reno, NV 89502. Tel: 775-829 2277
48. http://www.new-cancer-treatments.org/Articles/RootCanals.html

Chapter 20

The Benefits of a Coffee Enema Cleanse

The enema has been called "one of the oldest medical procedures still in use today." The Egyptian *Ebers Papyrus* (circa 1,550 B.C.), one of the oldest preserved medical documents known to be in existence, mentions it. While serving as a medic in World War I, Max Gerson, M.D., found that utilizing coffee rather than water for enemas had hitherto unknown healing and pain-relieving benefits for wounded soldiers. The caffeine in coffee administered as an enema detoxifies the liver. It is a natural treatment for cancer and other degenerative diseases.

No matter which degenerative disease is causing symptoms, the coffee enema will offer relief from confusion, general nervous tension, depression, allergy-related symptoms and, most importantly, severe pain.[49]

---

49. Gerson and Walker, "*The Gerson Therapy*"

"Once on the enema regimen, many people have noted a paradoxical calming effect, reduced stress and an overall restorative feeling.

"Organic coffee is a powerful agent for detoxifying. When used in enemas, it purifies the liver and its stored toxins."[50]

Since the enema is generally held for fifteen minutes, and all the blood in the body passes through the liver every three minutes, "These enemas represent a form of dialysis of blood across the gut wall.[51]

Dr. Lee Wattenberg was able to show that substances found in coffee—kahweol and cafestol palmitate—promote the activity of a key enzyme system, glutathione S-transferase. This system detoxifies a vast array of electrophiles [i.e. electron-lovers] from the bloodstream and is responsible for neutralizing free radicals—harmful chemicals now commonly implicated in the initiation of cancer.

God said:

Joel 3:21

For I will cleanse their blood ... .

According to Gar Hildenbrand of the Gerson Institute, coffee enemas "must be regarded as an important mechanism for carcinogen detoxification."[52]

---

50. Mechelle, Marie, articledashboard.com, *Natural Cure For Breast Cancer With Coffee Enemas*
51. *Healing Newsletter*, #13, May-June, 1986
52. https://enemacoffeereview.com/gar-hildenbrand-of-the-gerson-research-organization/

The Benefits of a Coffee Enema Cleanse

The Benefits of Coffee Enemas

- Aid in the elimination of the liver's toxic wastes
- Stimulate the liver's production of enzymes that cleanse the blood
- Draw out environmental and metabolic toxins
- Improve digestion and absorption of nutrients
- Cleanse the colon
- Improve the complexion
- Reduce puffiness around the eyes
- Improve joint health and flexibility
- Decrease congestion and allergies[53]

The coffee enema combined with a diet rich in fresh organic juices, fruits and vegetables and supplements has proven an effective method for combating breast cancer. By flooding the body with nutrition, while eliminating toxins, you boost the body's cancer-fighting ability, allowing it to heal naturally.

This treatment has so many health benefits that it should override any hesitation a person has to incorporate it into their regular hygiene program. The evidence is overwhelming: coffee enemas are an effective cure for cancer and many other serious health conditions. Traditional cancer treatment—chemotherapy, radiation and drugs—is devastating to one's physical and mental health and also to their quality of life.

Whether a person chooses to use this alternative approach to conventional medicine or simply as a

---
53. Ball, Jeanne, coffee-enemas.blogspot.com, January 27, 2009

supplement to help purify the system after chemotherapy, the coffee enema is a great cleanse that will help improve detoxification of your system.

Chapter 21

In Closing

Although it is not easy to restore one's health after a serious condition has manifested itself, it can be done. There are countless reports and research articles proving that proper diet, exercise, mental attitude, detoxification and faith in God's healing power combined are stronger than any disease.

I am a witness of this fact. In 2006 I was diagnosed with breast cancer. Through prayer, proper diet, exercise, rest and faith in God, my body was healed and today, thirteen years later, I am cancer free. You can be too.

Let me remind you of God's will in this matter:

3 John 2
Beloved, I pray that you may prosper in all things and be in health, just as your soul prospers.

AMEN!

Resources

- naturaldentistry.us/holistic-dentistry/ meridian-tooth-chart-from-encinitas-dentist/
- naturaldentistry.us/tag/acupuncturemeridian/
- extoxnet.orst.edu/faqs/dietcancer/homepage/cancer%20prevention.html
- beating-cancer-gently.com/
- FreeNewsletter
- cdc.gov/sleep/chronic_disease.htm
- allaboutspirituality.org/Christianmeditation-fq.htm
- thechristianmediator.com/
- new-cancer-treatments.or/Articles/RootCanals.html
- Marvin, Dr., Can Root Canals Cause Breast Cancer?, May 13, 2009
- Articledashboard.com/Article/Natural-Cure-for-Breast-Cancer-with-Coffee-Enemas/686057
- Aspartame: The Real Story, by Annemarie Colbin, Ph.D.
- foodandhealing.com/articles/articleaspartame.htm
- indigo.com/test-strips/ph-test-strips. html
- alkalizeforhealth.net/salivaphtest.htm
- snopes.com/medical/toxins/ aspartame.asp
- alkalizeforhealth.net/rebounder.htm
- psychologydebunked.com/ email0802_prescriptiondrugdeaths.htm
- scribd.com/doc/6635922/Natural-Cancer-Treatments
- townsendletter.com/Dec2007/ livercleanse1207/html
- forbes.com/2009/07/07/healthiestfoods-nutrition-lifestyle-health-heathiest-foods.html
- cmaj.ca/cgi/content/full/171/12/1451
- campaignfortruth.com/
- Eclub/200202/overdose.htm
- 4.dr-rath-foundation.org/THE_ FOUNDATION/News/2010/pharmaceutical_business/index.htm
- alternativehealth.co.nz/cancer/index.htm

Resources

- Reports from the University of Toronto (Clin Chim Acta, 235: 2, 1995, Mar 31, 207-19)
- Respected cancer researcher, Ralph Moss, wrote enthusiastically about The Grape Cure in the Spring, 1997, issue of his Media Watch
- mayoclinic.com/health/red-wine/HB00089
- winetastingguy.com/
- marksdailyapple.com/the-worldshealthiest-countries/
- U.S. National Institutes of Health, National Cancer Institute
- medicinenet.com/cancer/page2.htm
- busywomensfitness.com/exercisebenefits.html
- ctds.info/5_13_magnesium.htlm
- Dietary Reference Intakes for Water, Potassium, Sodium, Chloride, and Sulfate, available at nap.edu
- National Academies News Release, Report Sets Dietary Levels for Water, Salt, and Potassium to Maintain Health and Reduce Chronic Disease Risk, February 11, 2004, available at 8.nationalacademies.org/onpinews/newsitem.aspx?RecordID=10925
- Water and Nutrient-Rich Foods, The Sensible Way to Top Up Your Daily Water Requirement, available at brita.net/water_and_nutrient_rich_foods.html
- Jane E. Brody, Must I Have Another Glass? Maybe Not, a New Report
- Says, N.Y. Times, February 17, 2004, at FL
- Dian A Dooley, Ph.D., Water, Water Everywhere, available at islandscene.com/Article.aspx?id=2472
- Molly Siple, Juicy Foods: Need Fluid Fast? Drink Water. Otherwise, Foods With a High Water Content Can Provide Taste, Texture and
- Variety as They Contribute to Your Body's Reservoir,
- findarticles.com/p/articles/mi_m0876/is_n51/ai_8540811/Diuretics cause magnesium loss
- holisticmed.com/aspartame/recent.html
- wired.com/science/discoveries/news/2002/10/56072, Pancreatic Cancer treated with twice daily coffee enemas

- thoughtscreate.com/abccompete. html (E-book)
- life.gaiamcom/gaiam/ p/10WaystoDetoxifyYourBody.html
- healingcancernaturally.com/ thoughts-create-reality-links.html
- healingcancernaturally.com/healyourself-with-mind-power.html
- cancer.suite101.com/article.cfm/ does-chrysanthemum-extract-cure-cancer
- healingdeva.com/coffee_enemas. htm
- cancerfightingstrategies.com
- Murray, M. and Pizzorno, J. (1998). Encyclopedia of Natural Medicine.
- Rocklin, California: Prima Publishing.
- Carper, J. (1988). The Food Pharmacy. New York: Banam Books
- Hausman, P. & Benn Hurley, J. (1989). The Healing Foods. Emmaus,
- Pennsylvania: Rodale Press
- Duke, J.A. (1997). The Green Pharmacy. Emmaus, Pennsylvania: Rodale Press

Author Contact Page

For more information on ordering books or if you would like to contact Dr. Karen Drake to speak at your event:

E-mail:
DrKaren@PrimusUniversityofTheology.com

Web:
www.PrimusUniversityofTheology.com

www.ingramcontent.com/pod-product-compliance
Lightning Source LLC
LaVergne TN
LVHW040116080426
835507LV00039B/385